PUZZLE PIECES

A book of revealing

By Laurine Adams

Edited by Laurine Adams
Graphics by Laurine Adams

https://www.facebook.com/laurine.adams

About the author

Laurine Adams was born in Lexington, Kentucky, where she has resided all her life. She is the mother of five kids and grandmother of two grandsons. She believes every child has full potential and can ascertain any and everything, there is to have in life. She loves humanity and stands for the plight of the underdog. She thanks everyone who loved, helped and supported her along the way.

Puzzle Pieces

Puzzle Pieces is about a small girl, left to fend in life on her own. Having had all the negative dealt to her, in her beginning; she flipped the scenario and made life into a winning hand. This story rehearses how she persevered and overcame; to become all, generational cycles, dictated she could never be. The book gives insight to the powers that moved in her life and exhibits the things of the unseen. There is no way you can read this book without believing the uplifting results, of positivity.

Dedication

This book is dedicated to the only one in my life. My protector, provider, sustainer, and way maker. My savior, my comrade, my friend; that made me laugh, in the hardest of times. I love you with all that I am.

Contents

CHAPTER ONE

Framing the puzzle

Part 1

When I was only seven years old, I had my first profound dream. *In my dream, I saw myself running frantically. Around me, I could see black shadowed walls; and the place I was in, seemed like an eternity of hallways. I ran for what seemed like an hour, seeing nothing, but feeling a presence in the dark. As I ran, I would often look behind me, to see if what I felt was there; or if it had gotten close. I grew tired and felt so afraid. The me in the dream shouted. "Laurine, Laurine... please wake up. I became wearied, my breathing was sporadic and sweat poured from my head. I felt fear, in my mouth. My eyes caught sight of a light, coming from under a door. I ran towards the light and as I got closer, I saw a doorknob. I placed my hand on the knob, thankful that it turned. I pulled the door open; I had found a small closet. I went in, shut the door, placed my back to the wall and crouched. I waited to see if anything, from the dark, would find me. I placed my hands to my side, on the floor, to steady myself; as I crouched on my feet, with my knees bent. My left hand felt something wet. I looked down and saw a small, shallow puddle; that reflected my face. I saw a small girl, with long plaits, tears in her eyes. Her mouth had a slit, as she was gasping to breathe; and the strain showed in her tiny round eyes. I stared at her, as a tear fell. I had the realization; I was such a little girl. In the reflection, I saw the innocence, of a child. I closed my eyes and cried, then after I shed some tears, facts dawned on me. I realized, no one was coming to save that little girl in the puddle, that was me. I had to leave that little girl that was so fragile and vulnerable, behind; so that I could face whatever was out there. I looked again at the child, and said goodbye; then I disrupted the puddle, till her face faded away. Nothing small, weak and innocent could survive, what was lurking in the dark. I became brazen and pushed away tender emotions. I stood up, placed my hand on the knob, at turned it; then, I woke up.*

Upon awakening, I understood my dream. I was just a little girl. Life had been normal up to now, but suddenly, things had changed. I found myself at the age of seven, living in an unwelcoming community, living in a home with a dysfunctional family. Although I could see the dream, as if I was watching, three-dimensional, television; there were times I felt like I was there. I knew, the dream was right. To survive from this point on, I felt, I would have to stop crying, and muster the strength to survive. I would have to stay stern, put on a brazen face and not be deterred; as I watched my family become victimized, hopeless, and destroyed; by the taint; engulfing our world.

Currently I am forty-nine years old. My life has been an intense miraculous journey. Full of turmoil, disappointment and pain. I view my life in pieces, like a puzzle. My youth framed me. It is the outlier, of everything, I was destined to be. One might see a butterfly and remark of how beautiful it is. It's brilliant colors and majestic wings. They may gaze, as it flies, to higher heights; but what they don't realize, is that before it morphed, it existed in deep depths. When it was conceptualized and designed; it would first be a caterpillar. The depiction of how I see a butterfly, is the same depiction of how I see my life. How I started off in low places, found my way into a cocoon then morphed into everything I was ever designed to be. I want to take you on my life journey, it's path and all its stages. I feel I have a powerful story to tell, about everything- that was and should have been, but, in the end…wasn't. I want to share my enigma.

A puzzle has small pieces that fit together; to make a whole picture. My youth, from birth to eighteen, framed me. Everything that was necessary, to formulate who I would be, would happen here. I was born in 1970. I had a brother, a year and a half older, than I was; and a sister, four years older than

I was. There was the possibility of a younger sibling, but they didn't make it. I was marked, to not make it either, but I lived. Knowing that my fate had been set to be, my younger siblings' fate; tells me, I was destined to be. That one little fact will make so much of my life make sense.

My family: consisted of my mother, father, and siblings. When I was born, we lived in public housing. By the time I was six, my father had graduated college and moved our family to the suburbs. We were the first minorities, on our street. Once my father graduated, I was placed in a Montessori school. During this time, everything seemed so great. My father was very handsome, light tan skin, a nice afro and impeccable taste. He was very smart and had obtained a job as a systems analyst, at a big bank. Our move from public housing, was into a nice home, with beautiful furniture. I sat daily and watched my dad decorate. On one of the living room walls, that stretched about ten feet; my dad had put squares, of decorative glass, outlined with acrylic bricks. My dad was creative. Downstairs in the basement, my dad, had a room with a stereo, that reached wall to wall, and a floor model television, on the opposite wall. My dad had taken carpet pieces and glued them to make a psychedelic carpet. It was plush and multi-colored. The room adjacent was tiled in a dark brown print. There was a wood burning stove and closets, for yard tools and bikes. The room had a door that led outside to a big backyard, with a huge weeping willow tree. In the back of the basement was a game room, where I spent hours. I can still remember the nuance of the house. We had nice home, nice car and nice clothes. During the first year in the house, my siblings and I were sent to tennis and horse camps. We attended private Montessori and private Catholic schools. After the first year, there came a taint. My mom and dad argued more, and my father's behaviors were odd.

Going into the second year, in our home, I was verging on the age of eight. Things became crazy. My father was using drugs and alcohol on a regular basis. After he graduated and got a good job, he made more money. That money allowed him to start doing more expensive drugs, that caused him to be violent. One night while laying on my bed, I heard my father come in the house. He had been gone a few days. My mom was fussing, "where have you been! The mortgage money disappeared, the same time you did." My father slurred back. "get out of my face, I'm going to bed." The fight went on for an hour. My father became violent and I heard my mom yell, "what are you doing with that gun, put it down." My father retorted, "shut up and go to sleep". My mom ran off to the kitchen and called the police. The police showed up; I remember them coming inside and standing over my dad in his bed. My father got up and told the police, "get out, this is my house." My mother showed them the gun. The police asked him to leave the bedroom, so they could talk. My dad stumbled his way to the living room, where he became belligerent; the officer pulled out his night stick and hit my father in the head. My father fell, I remember the bright red blood, on the beautiful yellow couch. The cops handcuffed him and took him in.

I became accustomed to the violence, they fought anywhere, from the bedroom, to the front yard. Remembering the terror of watching my father beat my mom was traumatic. You never forget watching your mom being beat. It's like a horror movie when the monster is coming. You watch as the monster grabs its first victim. You are terrified of what will happen to the person as the monster drags its victim off. You wonder how awful that victim must feel or how afraid they must be. You stand motionless, torn between running for your life or doing something to help the one already caught. This is what it was like, when my dad; came home violent. My dad was a whole other man when he came home; after days of drinking, popping pills and doing drugs. His presence was tormenting, I disliked, when he came home, inebriated. I think my brother was more traumatized than me. I remembered one time, my brother stood between our violent dad and our mom. I was scared, for both.

After that night, with the gun; I began to rehearse, how I would escape my room, if my dad ever came for me; although the night he did come for me, I was in the kitchen.

About a year past my first profound dream; my dad had come home, once again, drunk, and high. My mom wasn't home. He came in the house; I was sitting in the living room. He looked at me, I looked back, at a wild man. He demanded; I fix him something to eat. “Get up and make me some salmon croquettes”, he said. I had never learned to cook, and he wanted salmon croquettes. I opened the can and dumped out the contents, into a bowl. I had no idea how I would take what was in front of me and turn it into the golden-brown patties my mom had often made. I wasn’t moving fast enough, so he smacked me in the head and told me to go wash the dishes. He was just standing there looking at me. I was scared. I turned and I ran. I opened the front door and took off. I ran across and up the street. I didn’t think, when I ran from my house, I just ran. I think all those nights rehearsing, paid off. When I got to the top of my street, I recognized a house. I had met two girls there one day, while I was riding my bike. The two girls were twins and had been outside in their yard playing, while their father was doing yard work. One of the girls had waved and asked me to come over to her. After a brief talk we jumped rope until I had to leave.

I ran up to the door of the twin's house and pounded on it, as hard as I could. It was late. I waited and pounded, in the dark. I turned to see my dad approaching and cried; beginning to think that no one would answer the door. Finally, I heard a sound of the door opening. I gasped, mouth wide open, and terror in my eyes. I looked up at him, saying nothing but desperation was all over my face. I saw a man at the door looking down at me. The same man that was doing yard work the day I had met the twins. The man looked up over my head as my father came up the path, that led to the door. I pushed my way in and stood behind him. My father said, “I want my daughter to come home”. The man responded, “she’s going to stay, here tonight.” My father didn’t give him any fuss; he turned and went away.

All, that night, I just sat there, on their couch. In the morning, when their mom got up, I asked her to let me out. When I got home, my dad was sleep. I went into my room and closed the door. My father had become a cruel man. Verbally and physically. There would come a time, I wouldn’t escape.

While I was in middle school, my dad had gotten a girlfriend; she called at night, while my mom worked, and before long, he decided to move out. He had come home one Christmas Eve, drunk, late at night or early morning. He woke my mom, siblings, and me, up; he told my mom to put up the tree. By now, he had lost his job at the bank, and was working odd jobs. While my mom put up the tree, I watched as my dad and sister talked. My sister was pouting; my dad looks at her and says, "now why are you mad?" "Out of all of you guys I've always loved you most, come give me a hug." Those words stuck with me. My dad always made it a point to let the world know my sister was his favorite. Those words would give me a complex of always needing to prove something. It caused me to have an oppressive mindset, never feeling as if I was adequate. If I had felt adequate, then I wouldn't feel as if I had something to prove. That night my mom and dad, sat and talked; with me and my siblings. My dad told my mom, he would be leaving. My mom took the news calmly and suggested my dad, take my brother; my dad made it crystal clear, he didn't want him. I was glad, my dad was leaving. He was no longer the man I had known, when he bought this house. The man I had sat every day and watched. I watched him put on his ties for work, I watched him shave and remembered the smell of his shaving crème. My dad, had left a long time ago, replaced by this man, who was leaving my mom. My dad's addictions were not my only horrors, but it was a relief, knowing he would be gone.

Part 2

My mom was brown skinned, like me. She was a beautiful woman, with a killer smile. My mom was raised on a different side of the tracks, than my dad. She grew up poor, but her family was close knit. My mother was very bright, she was a teacher; she didn't have a degree, but she had the skills. My mom could out sew and out cook, anybody. I was the black sheep of my family. After my father left, a great big piece of me was missing. I didn't have examples of my DNA and because of that, I had huge gaps in my identity. As a child I, watched my mom be ruled by depression. I watched as life was handled, being underhanded, cold and dishonest. For example, it was okay to do petty theft. Anytime a family member was in the hospital, it was ok to take washcloths, towels and blankets home. I watched my family talk about each other and tear one another down; then the next day smile in one another's faces. After offending, the matter was not addressed; no one was going to give the time, honesty or effort, to talk about it. Life was about self, not giving thought, to how our actions hurt or hindered others. We never dealt with or handled things; we weren't given knowledge, wisdom or instruction. I was not taught morality; I was not taught, being a lady or how to keep my body washed. The only talk I got from my mom, was when I got my period. My mom came and said, "now, you can't be screwing." I didn't know what screwing was.

My mom would go into bouts of depression. When she got sad, it lasted for days. She would go in her room, close her door and didn't want to be bothered. In time, the house became full of clutter and filth. The basement was the only place I had to watch television. One day I came home from school, went down to the basement and turned on the television. I turned around, to go and sit on the couch; and right above the long stereo, was a four-foot-tall by 3 feet wide, oil painting, of Satan. I stared at the picture, something in me was afraid, and I didn't return to the basement anymore.

Middle school through high school, was kind of quiet. I played basketball, for my middle school and high school teams. I didn't put a lot of effort into middle school. I was a thick girl, with uncombed hair and bad hygiene. In the ninth grade, I had a teacher, who told me I can do better. By my senior year, I obtained a great GPA and graduated top third of my class. I received a full, four-year scholarship, to a huge university; just because I believed, what my teacher had said. My senior year, I was also pregnant. I had hung out one night, heard a line from a guy; and that was all it took. I graduated in May and the baby was due in September. As I got closer to my due date, I prayed; to a God I never knew. I had never even thought about whether God existed, but that day I prayed. "God if you're real, please don't let my baby be born in this place."

We ended up having to move September 30th, due to the IRS taking our house; over something concerning my dad. At that point I was nine days overdue. The night after we moved out; I had my baby. Within three months, I had been approved for government housing; and I moved out, on my own. I didn't know anything about housekeeping, protecting my home or raising a kid. I had zero to no tools; to use in life. I had developed no character, had no financial knowledge, no direction, no instruction, no people skills, no spirituality, no form of religion. I didn't know how to drive; I didn't know how to go grocery shopping or pay bills. I had no determination, no foundation or reservation. The same soot that filled my childhood home, would fill mine; because the demons I ran from in my dreams, I was taking with me.

CHAPTER TWO

I'm Grown!

My mind was full of expectations, although I did not have any formulated plans, I just expected things to happen. My baby's father was long gone. I had decided shortly after high school; I didn't want to be bothered with him. I couldn't say why; there is no premise, it's just what I felt, at the time. I was just making moves. Whatever felt good, I wanted to try. I began to hang out with friends from high school, and drink. I was in college, but not attending college. For the next several years, I would squander men, along with time, opportunity and money.

The scholarship, I received, covered school; and I had plenty left over. I had welfare money, federal grants and I took out student loans. I don't know where the money went. The money certainly wasn't spent on books. I had no car; I paid no rent; I had no valuables. I was squandering my financial gains. During the first few years after high school, I was clubbing and regularly attending college parties. I met some good men along the way; but I didn't know the difference, between a jewel and lump of dirt. I was jumping from man to man; and before long; I had flunked out of college. By the time I looked up I had a whole new circle of friends; these new friends, came with new ways and habits. I started going to new places and being surrounded by new types of people. Six years after high school, I was sampling any and everything put on a table; that made me feel high, or gave me a buzz; until 1994, when I realize I was pregnant.

In my eager searching, I had found, bad debt, and endless hookups. I was wandering in the sea of life, with no direction; picking up any and every fishy thing I could find. Not knowing or understanding anything that was good. By the time, I had my second child, I was surrounded by strangers. People I knew nothing about. I was in a fast downfall. At nineteen I had my first child, by 24 I birthed my second. Right before I got pregnant with my second child, I met a handsome guy. I knew he was crazy, but he was the toughest, gang banger on the block; maybe, in the city. I figured I would be protected, in my neighborhood. He had come to my town, in the late eighties, at the age of seventeen, straight from the streets of Chicago. I had met him, the first time, in 1991, when a friend had invited him and some others to my place. I had no interest in him and paid him little attention. This was when I was still in college and hanging with the college crowd. After I had flunked out of college, I had started doing drugs. I wasn't focused on being a mom, my daughter was with family, most of the time. I spent my days hanging on the block, drinking forties and smoking cigarettes. At night, we would get inebriated and play cards. This was a daily event. In 1994, I would meet the guy from Chicago again; only this time he caught my eye. We weren't together long, before I was pregnant with my third child. I had started flirting with him weeks before I became pregnant with my second child. He was there for my second child's birth, but the baby looked nothing like him.

While pregnant with my third child, I caught my man cheating. I went home, took all his stuff and threw it down the apartment steps; went inside and locked the door. The next morning, I opened the door, sent my oldest, with a friend, to school. Before I could close the door, my man had his foot in it. I pushed him back and stood in front of the door. He let me know, I'm not going back in, without him. He pushed me, opened the door and we went in. He grabbed me, walked me to the bedroom and closed the door. He began to punch me in my arm repeatedly, in the same spot. Once I cried, he got up, walked to the bedroom door and went out. I sat there for about ten minutes, crying. He came back and began to punch me again. I yelled, "stop, you're going to make me lose my baby." He got up, stood over me, and began to swing a piece of metal at me; telling me I was not coming out. I became afraid and made a move for the bedroom door. He grabbed me, by my neck; and choked me till I couldn't breathe. After choking me, my third baby's father leaves the room and closes the door. I was afraid, I knew I must escape. It was just like, when I was young; but the roles had changed. I was the one in the room, crying; and my son sat in the hallway and heard me. I'm pregnant, but barely showing. I open the bedroom window and look down. I would have to jump from the second floor. I dangled my legs, held on to the ledge and dropped. The landing hurt. I see my man, look out the bedroom window; I get up and I run for my life. Some people, living downstairs; saw and heard me fall and came out to check on me. They brought me into their apartment and called the police.

My relationship was not the only thing volatile in my life, there were other things going on. One night, I was hanging with my girls. We pull up at the gas station and I got out. I went into the store, got something to drink and came back out. I saw two dudes standing at the driver's door. I rudely say, "excuse me," they let me slide behind the driver's seat and get in. I sit down and look up, at the two dudes, standing there. One of the guys is begging the other guy, "Not here, man, not here." The second guy has a gun. I see his finger on the trigger and my eyes follow the gun, to the barrel, which was pressed against my girl's forehead. The guy with the gun says, "man, this is her; she was with the dude, that shot at us." The first guy says, "yeah man, but don't kill her right here." I turn to the passenger side and saw another girl, that was with us; fifty feet away, inching backwards. I wonder if I should get out and run, but the guy with the gun listens to his friend and puts his gun up.

On another occasion, I was in the dope house, with my two kids; drugs are on the table. There was a knock at the door, and the owner shouts, come in. To our surprise, it's three policemen. There are four of us, at the table, playing cards; and one more person across the room. All of our kids are lying on couches. I jump up, to distract the police. I hold up my left hand and begin to speak; and with my right hand, I push the dope over, to a friend. My friend hides it, then he gets up and takes over. The police say, "we smell something," My friend says, "leave my house." One of the cops tells us, "we can take your kids tonight."

I wonder if it's so, but I stay calm. My friend talks the police down and they leave.

I have been in many dangers; but the day I was choked, made life and death, real to me. That day made me think. I realized I had hit rock bottom. I was devoid of character, I had a suspended driver's license, no job, no training, many habits, and was living in emotional and physical abuse; along with my two kids. I lived in public housing and still lived on welfare. I had been in gun fights, dope houses and places I don't remember. I had jumped from second story windows, pregnant, to escape from being beat. I had no goals and no ambitions. I began to wonder, what might happen to me, and became full of fear. I wondered if God was angry with me, and at that moment something profound happened.

I had been sitting outside on an upstairs, covered, deck. It was storming outside. Suddenly a bolt of lightning came down and struck the ground, about fifty feet from me. I became afraid, and wanted to run, but it was like something was holding me down. Immediately lightning struck behind me. I heard the sound. Then, I perceived a strong voice, that said; "if I wanted to kill you, I would have by now." I came to the resolution; if it wasn't my time to die, I must find some way to live.

My mom had been a battered woman. My dad had been an addict. I had grown up watching abuse, now my kids were watching. My kids had no protector, all they had was a caretaker. I was twenty-six and I was tired, of living a riotous life. I asked myself the question, “what is it, you wouldn’t do?” It’s one thing to know that your life needs a change; it’s another thing to know how to make that change.

CHAPTER THREE

My hero

It was 1997, I was twenty-seven years old and working as a waitress. I was still with the same man, that was beating me. He would watch the kids while I worked. When I got off, we would get high off my tips. Every time I got pregnant, I would quit using drugs and every time I went back to drugs the addiction, became stronger. When my tips weren't enough, we would sell something; or he would rip off the dope man. By this time, the oldest was eight. I had a son, who was two and another son, not even one. One day, the kid's dad left a package for me. I was getting dressed for work and every few minutes, I would take a hit. Before I knew it, I had done too much. I became sick and dizzy. The thought came to me, to go to the sink and rinse my nose with water; to try and dilute it. My heart was racing, and I sat down on the couch. It was scary, so I called my mom. I told my mom I was an addict, she asked "what do you want me to do?" Wanting to get free I called my dad's mom; she told me to call my mom. So, for the second time in my life, I prayed. "God, I don't want to be an addict, please save me."

One day in December 1997, I came home from work; the kid's dad told me, they had gone to church. He told me they would be going again next week. I got excited; I was ready to go. The Friday before we were going to church, the kid's dad came to me. He says, "I got another girl pregnant." I was angry; I didn't know what to say. I pouted all that weekend and come Sunday; he woke us up for church. I was sitting around not knowing if I would go, I wanted to spite him. He noticed my attitude and told me; he didn't care what I was going to do, but him and the kids were going to church. I pulled myself together and got dressed. Our ride came and we went to church.

At the church there was a man, he was called a preacher; and he would deliver a message called a sermon. The topic of the sermon was a way. A way to be washed, by faith, in the water of baptism. To be submerged and come up new. The preacher cried out to those that wanted a new start. He made a plea to those that wanted to give up their current ways and make a change. He spoke of a vehicle, named Jesus Christ, who was martyred, without sin, to become a sacrifice. He spoke of a God, that had seen people's conditions and wanted to free them. People bound in wretched ways, disabling conditions and bad habits. He asked the question, "is there anyone that wants to stop?" At that moment, I remembered my prayer. The second prayer I had ever prayed. Then he said, "Make your way this way." The preacher beckoned, those wanting to come out; to come to the front of the church. Without hesitation, I went. I didn't know anything that was ahead, but I knew there was nothing good in where I had been.

I was not baptized that day, but I was baptized the first Sunday of January 1998. That night after baptism, I had a dream. *I was in a place. It was dark there; and a figure of a man, came in and said follow me. The place was like a prison without bars. People were stuck and couldn't move; but nothing visible was stopping them. Everything around me was dark. I only saw shadows. I followed the man and he whisked me down some stairs, out the back door and into a hearse. The hearse doors were closed, and the vehicle took off. It drove down streets and around corners, to get me out. Then I woke up.* During that moment I didn't recognize the place, but it was a place that in time would become familiar to me. After the dream I was inspired to write this poem.

"HOPE"

I won't just be a master narrative and accept a cliché life. I want to experience blissfulness, for every pain I felt in my life. To visualize, that somewhere within me; are dreams that are buried within. To incorporate the unique fingerprints of God, on my situation. In the end, there won't be a sad story to tell; I would be an enigma; whose jubilee shines brighter than her hell.

While I was in a wretched condition, I heard a man preach; about a savior that healed all manner of sickness and disease. He opened, blind men's eyes. He touched lepers and restored, mad men's, minds

I was destined to be an addict, insane and living in hopelessness; according to my lineage; but this man was my game changer, he had already made a way. He would let me start all over and salvage my DNA.

I was baptized, the first week in January 1998; and married January 23rd, 1998. Somewhere between getting baptized and getting married, a pain in my abdomen took me to the emergency room. In the emergency room, they performed an ultrasound and found I was carrying two babies.

I began attending church. Bible class was a kind of school, where I learned scripture. I would hear things that encouraged me and helped me to see new things, outside of, what I was. The most significant thing I heard was, as a man thinketh so is he and life and death is in the power of the tongue. I began saying positive things. I began speaking things how I wanted them to be, versus accepting the way things were. I held on to the scripture that said, the truth will set you free. I began searching for all truths, even in simple things as that car is red. I began programming my mind with new thoughts and rehearsing scriptures throughout my day. I took notes in Bible class. Everything I was hearing was new to me. I learned to speak life to my kids, not ridiculing them, demeaning them or putting them down.

Around April of 1998, I learned my twins would be due, in August. I was having a boy and a girl. In May I felt heavy cramping and was taken to the emergency room. I was threatening to deliver. I was admitted to the hospital and placed on an IV of potassium. The potassium relaxed every muscle in my body. After being on potassium for a day, I couldn't turn my head or stop myself from drooling. I laid there for three days, in a complete haze. I went home and was placed on bed rest. I was prescribed medicine, to keep my body calm.

My husband had been doing well. For the first time in his life, he kept a steady job; and had bought a car. I was impressed when he changed the starter in the car, by only using a handbook. By July, I had been on bed rest for two months. I had missed a lot of church and wanted badly to be there. I had learned to talk often to God. I was rehearsing all the scriptures; I had heard at church and opening my Bible to study them. I had read a lot about faith. I had read, how God kept so many people and performed miracles. I wanted to try out, what I had read; and although it was impetuous, I went to the bathroom, stood over the toilet; and dumped out my pills, that kept my body calm. I told God I wanted to trust him. I wanted him to heal me.

The twins were due August 10th. By August 15th there were no signs of them coming, the doctor was a little shocked as most twins don't carry beyond full term. It is quite normal for them to come a little early. On August 15th the doctor scheduled me to be induced, on August 21st. I arrived at the hospital, in the early morning, on August 21st; before they could get me hooked up to inducement meds, labor had started. The doctor decided, my body was in labor and allowed it to continue by itself.

I was so proud bringing home my twins. We had moved out of the housing authority, after getting married; the housing authority, wouldn't allow my husband, on the lease. My husband was working and obtained a small straight back house, to rent. A straight back house is a home, that's very old and you must go through rooms to get to other rooms. There is no hallway. You enter the house, by the front door, into a room; you must go through the first room, to get to the next room. Through the next room, you entered a smaller room. After crossing through the third room, you get to the bathroom and kitchen, which sat side by side. The small house was full of mice. There was a big hole in the bathroom floor, which allowed the mice, to come in. There was an indication of mice, when we first viewed the house. I had not learned to head warning signs, so I never spoke up… I said nothing; and we moved in.

After the twins were born, my husband was not around much. Me and the twins stayed sick with the flu, for the next two months. My body was weak from having them; and they were tiny, with weak immune systems. It's amazing how the twins sustained. They were so tiny, with newly developing immune systems. The mice certainly didn't help matters. Later in life there was another indication, showing the twins were here, despite the odds. Late September 1998; I had a nine-year-old, who carried a lot of the load; since I was sick, and my husband was seldom at home. I also had a three-year-old, one year old- still in pampers, and newborn twins.

One day, in the first week of November, my husband told me he was giving a family member a ride. My husband never came back. It took me a day to realize he had taken the car and left. After a couple of days, of not hearing from him; I gathered the kids, put the twins in a stroller and walked to a pay phone to call his job. Luckily, he was in and I got to talk to him. He told me that he didn't want our new life, he said, I had to choose between him and God. I didn't have to think. I already knew I didn't want a life of drug addiction, hanging in the streets and being a horrible mom. I sat quietly on the phone, and he hung up. I was devastated, I lowered my head and walked the kids back home.

The next day, I walked to the health department, to see about getting the kids on assistance; to get their milk. While at the health department, I filled out a form, of things my household needed. On the form, I wrote down that we needed assistance with infestation of mice and a hole in the bathroom floor. When I got in, to see a worker; she approved me for immediate assistance, due to the circumstances. I had a great need. I had five kids and no income. I walked back home from the health department and for the rest of the day, I cried. The next day the housing authority sent a man, with poison, for the mice. Our landlord was contacted and told to fix the bathroom floor.

I had no idea what would come next. With no job, I had no way of paying December's rent. I had no car and a suspended driver's license. Thanksgiving, that year, was depressing. Before my husband left, he had applied for public housing. By the end of November his application was approved; and me and the kids moved into public housing. The time between Thanksgiving and Christmas, was hard. I remember lying in bed, one night, and telling God; that I wanted to commit spiritual suicide. I just wanted to give up the fight. I don't remember thinking anything else that night, the next thing I knew I was waking up, the next day, with a new determination.

Christmas brought, a little joy. A program had heard of my family's hard luck; and had asked, if they could submit our names, to be adopted for Christmas. I had agreed and two days before Christmas, I got a knock at my door. The knocker introduced herself and explained, she had a group of people, that wanted to bring our Christmas things in. I smiled at her and told her, “of course.” She turned to walk away and I my eyes followed. I saw three vehicles, parked outside our door. I watched, as approximately, five people emerged: out of their cars and a truck. They began to open their trunks and car doors. My eyes were teary, seeing the people carry, car seats, highchairs and play pens, by twos. They brought in boxes and boxes of household supplies; and cases of any and everything a family might need. Sheets, books and then toys. The things they brought in, engulfed, at least half of our living room. I was so touched. I was overwhelmed. I sat and looked at the things mounting around our Christmas tree and I cried. The kids had a wonderful Christmas. Although, I was in peril, these babies didn’t know what was happening. They opened toy after toy, robots, remote control cars, dolls and a multitude of teddy bears. My oldest had everything she had asked for and wanted.

Chapter Four

Figuring Out How the Puzzle Pieces Fit

Part 1

It was spring, 1999. I had found a rhythm to my life, a will to continue – and live. Around Christmas time, of 1998, I ran into an old friend. She was visiting one of my neighbors and came in to say hello. She told me; she had been at an event, where they were giving out Christmas gifts for kids. She had seen my husband; he had a new girl. I knew who the girl was, I had seen her several times. I had heard, thorough various people, she was with him at his families, for thanksgiving the same month he had left me. By February 1999, the news was they had moved away together. I don't know why it was important, but I filed for a divorce. I found a lawyer, willing to do my divorce, pro bono; by May of 1999, our divorce was final. I think it was part of my letting go and moving on.

The night of my divorce, when I slept, I had a dream. *In the dream I was inside of a room. In the room, I was fully grown and appeared to be my current age. The room had grey walls, and there was no furniture. I sat in the room; on the floor, with my legs crossed. The door opened and I turned to see; what appeared to me, the figure of a man. It was hard for me to see him, in entirety, as he was surrounded by light. The man had a broad chest and I saw him outstretch his hand. I got up off the floor, walked over to him and took his hand. We walked out of one room and into another. In the room, a family was sitting and interacting, but didn't observe us. I stood and watched the family. There were three children, on the floor, that appeared to be anywhere from seven to preteen. The children watched television while a man and a woman, were on a couch. I looked over and saw erotica, playing on the television, the kids were watching. The man was typing on a computer. I walked over to see, the screen. The man was typing, next to a username of BigDaddy; and someone with username SweetSugar, was responding. On the screen they were talking about what they did the other night. BigDaddy was telling SweetSugar, he missed her, and he was tired of his wife. I looked down and there was a small coffee table. On the table was a white substance and a razor blade, on a plate. My eyes drifted to the woman, that was with the man on the couch. She was lying, at the other end of the couch, covered with a blanket. Her eyes were open, but she wasn't looking at anything. I saw tears in her eyes, and her face appeared sad. I looked up, from the woman, because I heard one of the kids say, "I'm hungry". The smallest child had walked up to the woman. The woman didn't flinch or move her eyes. The child touched the woman, and told it again, "Momma, I am hungry." The mom responded, "I will be up in a while," never moving her eyes. The child replied, "but mom, that's what you said an hour ago." The child returned to her spot on the floor and laid down; she put her head on her arms and closed her eyes. The other two kids continued to watch television.*

My eyes found the man, that had brought me there, he reached his hand back to me and I walked over and took it. We exited the room through a door that led outside. Once outside, I looked back to see the place we had left. The place was a house. There was a wooden porch that was decayed. The house had a weathered roof, peeled paint and moss growing over the structure. The windows were blackened and had bars, and the structure seemed tilted; as if, at any moment it could fall. The man tugged my hand and I turned to him. We walked away, through grass, till we arrived at another place. This place had white siding and was upright. The house looked new. The man took a key and handed it to me. I unlocked the door and went in. Inside, the walls were painted white. I saw three rooms, all of them empty.

When I woke up, I got my journal and began to write down the dream. As I wrote, I had understanding. The place, the man came to get me; was a place of destitution. We walked into a room where I saw a family, plagued with erotica, drugs, adultery and depression. The house was a set of circumstances. The house was falling apart and unkept. The man walked me to a new place and gave me the keys. I now had a new set of circumstances; and it was up to me, what I filled it with. I now had a family and I wanted to give them everything good, as I discovered what good was. I wanted them to be safe and able to be children. No matter all chaos that happened outside our doors, chaos would not be in our home. I would pray and keep all evil out. There would be no hell raising, no cussing, no name calling. I would believe in marriage and wait on it. There was no drugs or alcohol in our home. We would watch tv as a family, eat together and take care of what we had. I was given the key to a new start. There would be conditions where kids felt free to exist and be vulnerable and loved. I would speak only what I knew to be truth, and practice giving my kids praise. Everything that was and should have been, according to generational cycles… would not be. We had a brand-new start, and it was up to us what our life would be.

It was August 2000. I had a five-year-old son and an eleven-year-old daughter, attending public school. I had two one-year old's and a toddler, who had turned two in April; that would be staying at home with me. I was so glad at least one of the three was out of pampers. At the time I was making $432 a month, on welfare. Diapers took a large chunk of that. My rent was free, and we received food stamps; so, I took a portion of the $432, went to a rent to own, and got a couch, washer and dryer. I had watched my dad furnish a home, but I had never seen a home maintained.

Outside of raising kids and tending the household, my mind was focused on how I think and behaviors. There's a lot of things I learned over the course of the next year. I had grown up exposed to and identifying with hoarding. I began imposing rules on my life. One major rule to defeat this trend was empty drawers and empty closets. If something is not being used; throw it away. I had a cold turkey, mentality. There would be no patty caking of any condition. Everything had a place. There could be no disorder. Keys, remotes, toys, clothes, papers; any and everything that was in our place, had a place. There was nothing allowed on the floors. Every day, everything must be picked up. No matter how much the kids played or misplaced, everything was to be placed back. Besides our home, I had to also get my mind in order, cleaned and situated.

I learned to speak plainly, without twisting or hypocrisy. I didn't speak with hidden meanings, or only revealing half of a thing. I learned to answer directly without talking to people in circles of confusion, avoiding the real question. I did all of this to free me, to situate myself with a foundation of truth. Before speaking clearly, I had to learn to think clearly. Sometimes we're taught misconceptions, or how to play dumb and naïve, when convenient. For instance, knowing everything about a situation, that doesn't concern us; but not comprehending when the situation is us, or we are being directly spoken to. Our first response is hah. When we respond hah, it's because we don't want to answer. We heard the person, but something blocked our minds from clarity or responding. We have tendencies to become deaf, suddenly.

I was taught, a lot of backward ways. As a child the adult taught, the child was to always speak and show respect, but the adult didn't. The adult could be as mean, rude and contrary; but that child, had best to be as respectful, as they could possibly be. So, as a small child, this behavior taught me hypocrisy. We learn to do unto others the opposite of what is done unto you. Once I went into my mind and caught the fallacies; I worked on a concept to replace it, thereby rewiring or remapping my mind. I learned that if I showed respect, the child mimicked the behavior. I never forced my kids or told them that they better speak. I don't believe in control, although I believe in discipline and reward. I formulated many ways to speak. Hola, nod of the head, a smile, or your basic hello. I taught with positive reinforcement. Something registered in my mind, one day; when I said, stop being bad. A I light came on; saying that doesn't teach them anything. I started telling them what they could have done positively, in that instance. I showed them repercussions rather than pushing what I say down their throats.

I was just learning new philosophy, a new language, if you will. New way of speaking, new aspects. I didn't know application or grasp an understanding. I didn't know the why's; I only began to pattern it, the best I could. Having three small kids, required a lot of my attention. Changing poopy diapers, all day, required a source of strength. I had to convince myself that I loved to do it. I had to find positivity, in the hardest things. I began to look at my babies as vulnerable little humans, they were not headaches; I would invest positive energy in them. I looked in their eyes; I spoke to them, at every age and I made connection. They were small, couldn't speak, couldn't defend themselves and didn't know right from wrong. They didn't understand much of anything. A child doesn't know if it's being mistreated, it only knows what it is given; but I knew. I had to be their protector; from things that were mean, hurtful or unkind. I looked into their eyes with love, and I sang to them. I stroked their cheeks and kissed their foreheads. Any frustration hurt or stress I felt; could not come near them.

The same gentle love I showed them, was being shown to me. I was grown but I was new. I had chosen to forsake all my old ways and learn everything over again. Learning ideology and gaining knowledge. All my principals were new, but in time, with application; my knowledge would evolve into wisdom. Along with gaining a renewed mind, I was ready to learn how to cook, clean, and take care of my hygiene. I didn't know how to be a mom, a friend, a wife; but I would develop values, using the Bible, as my guide. Me and the kids would learn this thing -together.

I began to have desires to have more. I began working on my credit. My student loans had defaulted; I also had a couple of unpaid credit cards, from when I was in college. I started paying $20 a month, credit card by credit card. I consistently paid for my, rent to own, furniture. By the time I looked up, another Christmas was passing. Come February 2000, I got a letter in the mail. My ex-husband had filed his taxes for the year 1999 and the government had kept the money. I was being notified, because in 1999 we were still married. The money was withheld, and the government used it to pay my student loans.

Somewhere around 2001 or 2002; I got a letter from welfare, that I had been placed on the welfare to work program. The sitting president had implemented welfare reform in August of 1996. The kids would receive free daycare and I was required to enter work, training, or volunteer; the government would pay for transportation. The first thing I tried was training. I went to a program that taught office skills. After completion of the program, they placed me on a temporary job, doing license plate, tag renewals. I was under a lot of stress. Waking up, getting kids dressed, putting two kids on the school bus, coming home and getting on the city bus; to drop three of the kids at daycare. I would then get back on the city bus and go to my job. Eventually the welfare to work program incorporated taxicab expense, but that took a while.

After office skills, I moved on to doing culinary training, which led to a job, in the school system, as a lunch lady. Come 2003 all the kids were in school. I began looking into going back to school. It had been twelve years, since I was in school, so the school I applied for; allowed me to do academic bankruptcy. Academic bankruptcy allowed me to keep all the credits I had earned, in my teens; but erase my GPA. The school I would be attending, was a community college owned by the big university; I had attended after high school, therefore my credits transferred easily. My student loans were in good standing and I was ready to start college.

By 2003 I had read the Bible two times and become a Sunday school teacher. I had kept up a strong prayer life. Raising five kids, alone, wasn't easy. We were extremely poor; we made ways to have family time, laughter and fun. During the summers, we walked downtown and played in the town fountains. We couldn't afford cable, but we got a DVD player; and walked to the public library, to rent movies. In 2004, I qualified to finance a van. I had gotten my license by going downtown, paying a fine and having it reinstated. Once we had the van, we would go to a large park on Fridays, during the summer, where they played free movies. I was all the kids had. No one else wanted to be part of our family. They did not embrace the changes I had made.

There were some trying times on top of my time of trying. Put that together and you have tribulation. One night I dreamed a dream. *In the dream, I was in a place, not sure where. In this place, there was darkness all around me. There was light coming from a window; about 200 feet straight ahead of me. In the dream a voice said, "open the gates." Immediately water started pouring in. I saw myself in the dream, my head went under water. Then a voice whispered, "endure, I will bring you out."* I woke up and wrote down my dream. From 1998 to about 2003 life was full of turmoil. The first thing that comes to memory was a murder. It was early morning. I had sent all the kids to school and I was getting dressed, to go to work. I heard something loud from outside. I started to walk to the kitchen window, but I delayed and stood there. A couple of minutes passed, and I went to look. Sitting in a car, about two doors down; I saw a woman, she was dead. Her hand was hanging out the window, her mouth was wide open, and her head was tilted to the left. The police came, but the killer had got away. Months later, I was home taking a nap; I heard a pop, like a cap gun. I sat up, unsure of what I had heard. I didn't think much about it. Shortly after, I got a knock at the door. The police wanted to know if I had heard anything. I told them I wasn't sure, but I thought I had heard a pop. They said they are investigating, but it appears, a man next door, had killed himself.

A few months after the murder and the suicide my car windows got shot out. Shootings happened every other day outside of our dwelling. It wasn't safe for the kids. My kids often struggled in school. Kids that see shootings, prostitutes, addicts and drug dealers- daily; don't have the same things on their minds, as other kids. My kids had multiple struggles, the biggest was only having me. After work and school, I didn't have the energy they deserve. Because of this their homework suffered. They had many odds against them. Not only was I a single parent, with five kids; we lived in a lowly environment with lots of chaos, and danger. Although stress should have had a grand impact, I was surviving. My prayer life was my peace, and God's word, my power.

Whereas my eyes, used to yearn, for something to appear before them; now I realized I needed to make things happen. I had direction and focus. I wanted to be self-sufficient and I wanted a place, that was safe and roomy; for me and the kids to live. If I didn't make life happen, then life would happen to me. In 2002, I started my lunch lady job; by 2003, I had transitioned off welfare and started college. In 2004, I graduated with my associates, in the summer; and started substitute teaching in the fall. I had two kids in the first grade, one in second, one in fourth; and my oldest was in middle school. I felt so proud when I got assignments, to teach at my kids' elementary school. Me being there as a teacher brought joy, not only to my kids, but kids in our neighborhood, as well. It was a phenomenal feeling, putting my kids on the bus, at the housing authority. Going home, getting in my car; and driving to their school to substitute teach. It was surreal, being that just four years prior; I was an addict.

I was seeing progress amongst tragedies. One night I woke up to my cell phone ringing. A church member and neighbor asked me, what was happening. I didn't know what she was talking about. She told me to go outside and look, in the front parking lot. I walked outside, around a set of apartments and saw people everywhere. As I got closer to the commotion, a young man was walking around in a circle, saying, "I tried, I tried to help them." I got closer and I saw a fireman doing CPR on a woman. I will never forget how hard he was doing chest compressions to her lifeless body. That night two kids and a mom died in a fire. I saw them remove one of the kids on a couch. One child lived. The man walking around had tried to get in to save them, when he heard the mom screaming from a window.

There were other tragedies and many other murders, but over time these things became commonplace. It is remarkable how God kept my mind. We had many neighbors, that were living the life I once had. I was in the midst of, but being kept from; all the drug use, partying and things going on, at night. All around me, were moms who were addicts, with lots of kids. I always tried to convey to my children, that that's where, they would have been. We were Protected, in a dangerous environment. One night I fell asleep, on the couch. Our dwelling had two floors. All the kids were upstairs; that night I woke up, around two in the morning. I walked to the kitchen, but I didn't know why. At that moment my back-door's knob turned, and my door began to open. I ran to the door, slammed it shut and locked it. Many times, we were outside in gunfire or close to a murder. I used to be the biggest punk. Now I had to be the guarder of my home. If I heard a noise, I didn't lie there and wait till danger came upon me. I got up searched out the noise and faced it. I was not a victim; I was the victor.

One day, before we had a car, I left the kids with the oldest and walked to the neighborhood store. Our neighborhood had the highest crime rate, in the city. After leaving the store, I saw someone following me, very close behind. They were so close to me; they wouldn't have to reach far, to touch me. I didn't know what his intent was. I stepped up on a concrete block, in a parking lot; with one foot. I spun around, and nose to nose, I looked him in the eye and said, "what do you want?". The man was thrown off, he stepped back and made his way around me. I was learning in the natural but preparing for the spiritual.

Part 2

When things got heavy, I remembered the dream and I would cry and believe that he would bring me out; I was determined to endure. The water, in the dream, symbolized trouble. Troubles that went well over my head. The fears and traumas and demons, I faced as a little girl, had trained me in a couple of things. The first thing I knew without a doubt, was that evil was real. So, once I began my journey, for a new way and life, I knew I had an enemy. When you know you have an enemy, you don't take things lightly or for granted. When I was a little girl, I didn't know how to fight so I succumbed. Because I had succumbed, by high school, I wasn't running, in my dreams anymore. Between 1998 and 2004, was a time of war. This time when demons came in, I knew how to endure. When depression came in, at night, to remind me how alone I was; or told me to give up, I prayed. I steadied my mind till depression left. I rehearsed the word of God, reminded myself that he loves every one of us and is close to those with a broken heart.

When poverty had a firm grip and carnage was surrounding us. I pressed my way and asked God to cover us. My shield (faith) and my sword (word of God) are all I had. My shield and my sword brought us through. Loneliness can be a beast and push us to find anyone to hang with; or anything to do. In the face of loneliness, I stood still and remained firm, that I would rather be alone; than doing anything outside of God. My truth became the Bible. If the bible said it was good, then I said it was good. If the bible said it's wrong, then I framed my mentality that it's wrong. All the negativity, I heard as a girl, I came against -with continuous praise. I found something good to say about any and everything. I refused to see the bad. If my whole day was full of kids, messes, hard days at work, discipline, balancing finances, strategizing; or scheduling doctors' visits, dentist appointments or teachers' conferences; then I focused on being thankful for health, strength in my body, kids to love and a job to go to. I learned to speak to people, open and honestly, even if it was to my embarrassment or shame. I learned to tell on myself, when I had bad thoughts or incorrect perceptions; of something someone did. I would not manipulate and scheme and flip, according to my agenda, or to make myself look and feel better. I learned to face myself; and that takes power. Of all things, I learned to be honest about; the biggest truth's I saw, were of myself. It's impossible to eradicate, things in you, if you won't face and admit that it exists. I learned to face my fears and not run from them. I had always loved highs, whether it was roller coasters, joy riding in a stolen car or drugs; but now Gods word was my dope and praising him was my new high.

Part 3

I wanted my kids to have ethics. I was determined my kids would always have each other. I branded it in them and always uprooted petty things. They were not allowed to pick on or tease one another, in my presence; but of course, they would joke or have light banter. Any signs of jealousy or pettiness got a stern lecture. There was a time, when all six of us climbed into and slept on a twin bed. We were close. I always spoke to them positivity. Although their dads were gone, I never spoke bad of them. I told them the fun things and the strong things about them. All people are born with talents and gifts; and have it within them, to be unique and powerful. It is our ways, attitudes, perceptions and character, that get messed up; but there are things, within us, that are redeemable. I needed them to see the good in them, so they had to see the good in their dads. I never wanted them to feel odd, weird or left out, because they weren't seeing those parts of them.

I spent some years, working on me. Unlearning, most things, and reprogramming. Creating new pathways in my mind, with the word of God; so that things connected and led to good places. My frame was developed, to counteract, things done to me, taught to me or shown me, in my youth. Upon that, I continued the puzzle by implementing things, I had never learned or heard. I devised a code of ethics and behavior; of how we would treat one another. I talked to my kids about everything. Showing them my weaknesses and concerns, so they would learn to show theirs.

Me and the kids were growing together. We were building on the frame of our puzzle. I wanted to offer them the best of everything. To me everything wasn't money. I saw my father obtain financial wealth, and it didn't make a happy home. I wanted my kids to have the best of being loved and the best of examples; of how to flourish in life, and as good human beings. I taught the kids good character, good morals, good attitudes and values. I wanted to offer them hope and positivity. We were in poverty, living in carnage, and destitute, but they didn't know it. They learned how to laugh, love and dream.

I had told you earlier of a dream; about a man leading me to a hearse through which I escaped. A hearse is a vehicle. A vehicle is a mode of transportation, to take you from one place to another. A hearse symbolizes death. In the dream I was seeing that I must die in Christ, and through his death, a way of escape was created. The escape was happening, when I learned to fight, when I learned all the trickery that was handed to me, to keep me down. It was a process. When Jesus died, he went through a process and he had work to do, for three days. I too had work to do to complete the process of escaping via his death, and he had shown me the way. Once I escaped the identity, I had once had; I was ready to learn a new life. So, as a baby; his word fed, taught and showed me a new way.

Chapter Five

Transitioning

In 2004, I had completely repaired my credit. I applied whatever extra money I had, from five dollars to twenty; to one delinquent bill at a time. Eventually, each bill, had been paid off or settled. In January of 2004, I purchased a 2003 dodge grand caravan. The kids were so excited; they no longer had to squeeze into a car. A lot of things were beginning to change. The church I attended, was breaking up; and the projects, we were living in, were being torn down. 2004 and 2005, went by in a flash. I was looking for places to live. We were looking for subsidized housing, in the form of a house. Due to the projects being scheduled, to be torn down; the government was paying to relocate everybody. I looked but couldn't find a place. In 2006 the church was collapsed, and it was time for us to move. I had to settle on a sideways move. We were moving into another government housing project. This housing project was smaller, but the dwelling was much bigger. Being it was a more condensed area, shootings and murders always happened, right outside your door.

I started working a second job as a telephone operator and eventually stopped substitute teaching. Substitute teaching only allowed me to work when school was in session. I tried working in janitorial for the schools during the summer; but that hadn't worked out well. Within months as an operator, I had been promoted to work in the supervisor queue. My pay didn't increase, but I had minimal calls. I studied the bylaws of the company, I answered phones for, and became knowledgeable; in how to handle most matters and assist customers.

I had been so focused raising the kids and working, to get out of poverty, that I had not had time to even think about a man. During such a crucial and pivotal time of developing positive things; in me and my kids' life. It could have been detrimental inviting in new things. Finding someone is a process and in that process, you can encounter tainted beings. I didn't want anything coming in and disrupting the balance of positive things going on in our lives. All my energy, for the past eight years, was focused and directed. My oldest daughter was now in high school. When she left middle school, a plaque, with her name; was placed in the principal's office. The award recognized her for being an exceptional person and was called, the Coretta Scott King award. When we made the move from one government housing project to the next, she was ready for her senior year. She wasn't at home very much. When all the kids had reached grade school, I allowed her to stay with a friend, on weekends. By the time she reached her senior year; me and the smaller kids had a handle on things, freeing my oldest to stay with her friend as much as she wanted. I didn't want her in the home, with so much struggle, suffering. I wanted her to have, so much more. I wanted to carry the weight. I had the kids and I refused to allow the burden to fall on her. All my kids were very close. I taught them to be there for each other. My oldest daughter had done so much for me, I had promised her a house. I don't know what I would have done, if God had not allowed me her. One amazing thing about God; even when you don't know him, he still knows you and is moving on your behalf.

In 2006, I had one senior, one middle schooler, and three still in elementary. The school year came and went, and in 2007, I had a high school graduate. I picked the theme of a luau, and we had a big barbecue. Around this same time, some of my neighbors were getting new housing. The projects we had moved out of, had been rebuilt, into beautiful townhomes. My family wasn't chosen to get one. I did cry a little and wonder why we weren't chosen; to move into one of the homes, but I had learned to trust God. Remembering all the things that had taken place in the past eight to nine years; allowed me to peacefully trust the process. I had always wanted to provide my kids a place that wasn't congested and dangerous. My daughter had grown up, before I got that chance. We loved on my oldest; to let her know how proud we were, then it was back to business as usual.

I loved bible stories; they encouraged me. The stories helped me to realize, there were many that had hard times. There were many in the bible going through rough experiences, that left them wounded or rejected. Having five kids caused a lot of rejection and ostracizing. Most people weren't glad to see the woman and her five kids, show up, at any event. People look at you a certain way when you live in the projects. Single mom, living off government assistance, with five kids; equated to a scourge on society in a lot of people's minds. Some teachers and principals had no expectation, of you or your kids. I admit, we weren't perfect. We didn't look perfect, but we lived in gentleness and love. I had to keep my kids close to me, because people tended to sneer, or mistreat them, when they weren't in my sight. They might have thought it was so unfair, but I didn't let them run and play at gatherings. I know my kids were a little rough and hyper. Most people didn't want to be around them; but I loved them. They were my heart and the reason I worked so hard.

In August of 2007, I decided to apply for a house; through a program that builds houses for qualifying families. I applied but didn't qualify. I had taken on a little debt and needed to go back to the plan that got me out of the hole before. Spring of 2008, the same program had a booth set up, across the street from my job. I walked over on my lunch break and picked up a flyer. A lady asked if I was interested. I explained I had applied last year but was denied. She encouraged me to try again. I picked up a form, filled it out, and handed it to her. Within two weeks I got a letter that we were approved. My oldest had moved out of the home, so it was me and the four kids.

By the end of 2008 I had my property picked out, floor plan made and the start of building date. I was on cloud nine. Building would begin the start of spring 2009. My van was one year from being paid off; it seemed like it was time to run my last stretch into nirvana. Around Christmas of 2008

I had a dream. *I was in a place. The lighting was as a grey cloudy day. I walked around and I looked at the scenery. The place looked like an army base. There were bunkers and pavement linking them. The place was surrounded by a twenty-foot metal fence. An alarm sounded, I turned to see a great storm. I ran to a bunker and went inside. During the storm there was something I was seeking for; I was trying to find a key; so that when the storm was over, I could leave.*

When I woke up, I wrote down the dream. I understood the place, as the one from my dream before, where I was in the many waters and they went over my head. I had come a long way. I had endured the waters and an amazing place had been built. The time me and the kids had spent, in the first projects, was like a war zone. I had endured, we had survived. The word of God had fenced us in, and prayer had been my bunker. The pavement represented ways that had been made. The only part of the dream I didn't want to face, was the storm. Hadn't we been through enough. Hadn't we overcome. No matter why this was happening, I took heed, and went into a routine of prayer. The only part of the dream I didn't understand, was searching for a key. Why was I searching and what did the key mean? I only knew in the dream, that once the storm had passed; I couldn't leave that place without it.

2004 I started to notice a transitioning of seasons. I had endured tribulation and in 2004 turmoil started to slow down. As I eased into a new season, I began to see a hint of new things and life wasn't as pressing. The bible says, to everything there is a season and a time for everything done under the son. I didn't know what my new season was, but I saw change. By 2006 the church I attended, had broken up and my family had plans for moving into the next housing project. A hint I had into my new season was a scripture God gave me. The scripture was about a man named Peter who wanted to walk on water. Peter's faith carried him onto the water, in a storm; but when a boisterous wind sounded; Peter fell, and Jesus saved him.

Chapter Six

Mass Confusion

The time was approaching, for us to move into our new home. It was a four-bedroom house, with a moderate amount of land. I was still working as a telephone operator. For the year of 2008, I was awarded for being the top performer in all metrics. Call efficiency, absenteeism and break adherence, quality scores, and system functionality. I was given two thousand dollars, in 2009, for the accomplishment. I put the money in savings. September 2009, we moved into the house. The money I had in savings bought furniture for the house. The home came equipped with kitchen appliances, laundry room appliances, and a Posturepedic bed. The rest of the furniture such as dining room set and living room furniture, I purchased. The old furniture was battered and torn; the old washer had washed its last load. As usual, the timing for the award, was perfect.

Some may wonder why I would thank God for all of this. I thank him, for the perfect health; that allowed me to be at work every day. I thank him for the strength, it took, to participate in building our house, getting the kids to school, making sure kids had dental checkups and medical checkups, attending parent teacher meetings and taking care of our home; while still making it to work. I am grateful, that one day my mind opened to understand the system; and I saw how to keep perfect metrics. I'm thankful my car didn't break down, never got a flat tire, and everything worked out. Although I must confess, my stress was at an all-time high. I wasn't so young anymore. By the time we moved into our home I was thirty-nine.

The kids, still at home, were fourteen, Twelve and eleven. My twelve-year-old, was focused on everything, going on, in the streets. He wasn't attending class, although he was getting on the bus, to go to school. He was disappearing from home and not focused in school. I was at my wits end. I prayed and one night I had a dream. *In the dream, I was sitting and crying, holding on to my twelve-year-old baby. A white cloud was over me, and from it I heard, give him to me. I took my son and placed him in God's hand. I heard a voice say, you are his mom, not his savior. I watched as the hand lifted my son and took him away.* I woke up, to a knock at the door. When I answered, to my surprise; it was my sons, fraternal grandmother. She was saying hi and bye, to the kids, because she was leaving. She was going to Arizona. Without thinking, I told her to take my son to his dad, who was now in Arizona. She said she would be leaving in the morning on a bus. I told her I would meet her there; he would be ready. I cried, I vomited, I prayed. Never had my baby, been away from me. I made up my mind, I couldn't send him alone. My twelve-year-old wasn't alert, but I had no doubt in my mind that his eleven-year-old brother; could get dropped off in the desert and make it back home. I decided to send them both. I sent the eleven-year-old to protect the twelve-year-old and get them home if he needed to.

I packed their bags, winter of 2009, put them on greyhound and they left. Every day I cried, and I threw up. I was pressing my way to work, but not with the same ferventness. I was devastated. I called them every day, and after two months my eleven-year-old was ready to come home. My life consisted of long days and long nights. Not a day went by that I didn't vomit once or twice. I questioned myself every day, if I made the right decision.

By spring of 2010, the kid's dad was moving to Illinois. The moment they got there; I was on the highway to see my boys. My eleven-year-old wanted to come home. I was so glad to be driving him back with me, but him being there with my other son; gave me the peace I needed to sleep. My eleven-year-old girl and my fourteen-year-old, were mellow. They were doing great. I went back and forth to Illinois every month. I noticed my son spent most of his time at strangers' homes. His dad didn't have a job and his dads' girlfriend was taking care of him. My twelve-year-old turned thirteen in spring. By the end of summer 2010, something changed. I was no longer allowed to talk to my son, without his dad on the phone. When I went to visit, there were strange people around the home. It had been ten years since I had been around their dad; the more I went to visit; the more things came back to me. Then, one day, it all became concrete. The language he spoke, the people knocking on the door. I began to remember all the things he used to do and realized he's still doing them. Once I realized, he had not changed, and remembered exactly who he was; I knew it was time for my son to come home. I figured it would be better to fight him, out of the streets, than the streets being his home. I made up a reason for him to come back home, his dad agreed; but a family member got into his ear and started a fight. The next time I called, his dad told me I could try and come, if I wanted to. I knew him, and I knew it was a threat. All the domestic violence episodes clouded over me and I went into anxiety. I began to remember conversations; of things I knew he did in the streets. I knew if I showed up, I would be beat, humiliated and sent home. Men like him only understood police or a gun. Just having a gun wouldn't scare him, a person would have to pull the trigger.

His threat took me back to the years of being beat. I was in complete fear, of what he may do to me, but it dissipated to the thoughts of my son. I had my youngest son; call his dad and he got his brother on the phone. I got on the phone and I told my son. “Momma won’t be there for a while. I need you to take care of yourself. If your allergies come, you go in the bathroom and turn on the shower.” “Let the hot water run a while, while you breathe; so, you don’t go into pneumonia.” He had once gone into pneumonia, as a kid. I had learned he got allergies every year. The allergies would run into his chest, and he would cough all night. For once, I needed him to take care of himself, because I could not be there, to stop his drainage. My baby had been gone almost a year, I had to find a way to get him home.

I had never been a violent person, so I sought a way; that I could take the police. I went to legal self-help, in the courthouse. I went in and a man was standing in the lobby. He said can I help you. My whole situation poured from me. Although the man couldn't give me legal advice, he talked me through it. I learned that my, Kentucky, divorce decree, giving me custody; wouldn't work in Illinois. I learned, the police wouldn't be able to help me, unless the decree was entered as Illinois law. So, I went home, and I cried. I fell asleep and I had a dream. *In the dream, I sat on a rock, looking at a river. The sky was grey, and I sat alone. I heard the water crash against the rocks and saw the waters downstream, were in a violent storm. Within moments, the storm made its way overhead, and engulfed me, but I didn't care. I just sat there. I felt a presence, and I looked to my right side. There, sitting with me, was a figure of a man, as a shadow. This time, there was no shining light around him. He sat close, and after a while, he said, "you're angry."* I woke up not understanding my dream, because, every day I gave God thanks. "Thank you for my health, thank you for my home, thank you for my job"; but the man said I was angry.

I searched my feelings and talked to God. I told him "when my husband left, I trusted you. When we couldn't find a place and remained in the projects, I trusted you. I've trusted you now, for twelve years, and yet; here I am suffering, the most hurt, I have ever felt. When does trusting you pay off, how much must I endure?" At that point, I got up; I walked to a shelf and within five minutes, I had broken everything I could break, in my living room. I shouted, "My son is not here, and yet you haven't said a word!" then I heard a voice, whisper, "you are angry without a cause."

The next day, I had a mandatory appointment. The county attorney's office wanted me to come in, about child support. I went into my paralegal's office and sat down. The paralegal was telling me, they were going after the kid's dad, in Arizona. I explained to her, he's not in Arizona. She kept speaking, as if she had not heard me. I said loudly, "Lady, this man has kidnapped my son, if you don't have a way for me to enter my divorce decree into Illinois, I'm done talking to you." She asked me to hold on and please sign some papers. I sat there, while she finished typing, then she started printing, what she was working on. As the papers printed, the office door opened. A lady came in, looked at me and said "ma'am, I overheard you, and I did some digging. Those divorce papers were entered, in the state of Illinois, back in 2005. We had sent them, when we had indication your ex-husband was working there." I looked at the woman, I stood up, then fell to my knees and cried, "thank you! Thank you so much." I went home gassed up my van and prepared to leave in the morning. My youngest son helped me with the landscape and gave me the name of the school. I called Illinois, and after a back and forth, verified the divorce decree was there. I got instructions on how to pick it up. I then called the school and spoke to the sitting principal, who also happened to be the superintendent. I told her I was coming to get my son, then I hung up.

The next morning, I plugged the coordinates, they gave me; to get a copy of my divorce decree, into my GPS and I was on my way. It took six hours to get there, I had left home at 2 am. I first went to the courthouse, and picked up my divorce decree, that was now Illinois law. On the way out of the courthouse, I stopped and told some police officers, what I was going to do. They said, the school will call, if they need us. I got in my van, plugged in my sons' schools' coordinates and I was on my way. I pulled up to the school, clutched my decree, in my hand; and walked in. I went into the office and told the desk clerk; I was here to pick up my son. She got my sons name and called for him to come down. I told her thank you and walked out into the hall. In a couple of minutes, I saw my sons face. His dad had threatened me in the summer; it was now October. My son hesitated when he saw me, so I reached out my hand. He walked up to me, took my hand and we left. The desk clerk hadn't asked me for anything, not even my ID.

I got into the van and my son said, "dad is on his way to come get me." I asked why and he said, he had an appointment for a physical. Knowing his dad could show up, rattled me. I told my son, it was okay, and we left. I got lost, taking a wrong turn, then my son helped me. Once I saw my way, I took a turn left, when he told me to turn right, to get to his dad's house. When I kept going my way, he became afraid. As I entered the highway, he placed his hand on the door and opened it, as if he was going to jump. I grabbed him, pulled him back and yelled, “close the door”. He did, and we drove on. After an hour, I pulled off the highway, to get him something to eat. I was hurt, that he had opened the van door as if he wanted to get away from me. I turned and looked at him. He sat with his arms crossed, defiance on his face. As if I understood, the first thing I said was, “you’ll never have to see him again.” He looked at me and his eyes said, really, then a tear rolled down his cheek. I said, I will go to God; that if he ever bothers us, God will step in. My son cried, I held him, then we went into eat.

As we ate, we both were quiet. We finished our food, then continued our journey home. The next morning, I got in the van to go to the kids' school, to enroll my son; whom I had brought back home. I got in the van and it wouldn't start. It was completely dead. I took out the keys, walked back into my home and called the school; to see what I needed, to get him enrolled. The school told me, they needed his records from the school in Illinois, to ensure he's being placed in the proper grade. I hung up and called Illinois. I told the person that answered the phone, what I needed, and I gave my son's name. The lady asked me to hold a second. Another woman picked up the phone and asked if I was my sons' mom. I told her yes. She explained that his dad showed up, after me, and he had told them, I had no right to pick him up. She went on to say, that he called the police and demanded they issue an amber alert, but because I had called, she asked the police to wait. She asked me, would I please send the divorce decree to her and I agreed. I got her information and she got the schools information; so, I could fax what she would need, and she would in turn; fax what I needed, for the school.

Part 2

After that was taken care of, I got onto the couch and sat there. I began to rehearse in my mind, all the things we had gone through and wondered what it was all for. I kept my son close to me, and every chance I got, I held him in my arms. He had always been my challenge. He was the reason I prayed and cried many nights. I went to bed that night and I had a dream.

In the dream I was a caterpillar. I was tiny and crawled around in dark places. There were many caterpillars there, in what appeared to be crevasses. I poked my head outside the crevasse and saw spiders. I felt curious, so I went into a spider's lair, while the spiders weren't watching me. The lair was amazing and one lone spider inside was spinning a web. The spider finished its task, then beckoned me. I was so amazed; I began to go closer, but, just before I reached the beautiful white creation, I felt a tug in me. There was a pull, as if on the inside, and I began to follow it. I crawled, out of the lair; higher up the tree, onto a limb and I hung upside down. Magically a substance began surrounding me, I felt like I couldn't breathe. The substance became tighter and tighter, till I couldn't move or see. I sat there motionless, afraid. There in that place, all I had, was my mind. Everything was completely dark and quiet. Every now and then I felt pain all through me. It felt like something was stretching me and bending me. I cried out but didn't make a sound. Oh, the pain, the darkness, the quiet; was unbearable. I screamed again, but nothing came out. I wanted so much to be free. After much pain, the sensations in me subsided. I just sat there in the quiet. Suddenly I heard, "mother of a nation". I chased the sound with my mind, running after it in my thoughts. Wondering, who it was or where it came from. Then, once again, total silence. In time, I thought I was going to lose my mind. Where is this place; what is this, that is happening to me? Then I heard, "a support to your husband". After that I, heard nothing else. I pondered what could these words mean. I echoed them to myself. In time, a fingertip appeared; and begin to draw colorful lines. The fingertip was beautifying me. When the fingertip was done, I saw a small beam of light. I pressed my way to it but couldn't move. I pressed again, and nothing. I remembered the words I had heard, and it inspired me. I continued to push, then finally I felt something give. I pushed for hours, until I was free. I sat there observing my surroundings and listening to sounds... then the dream ended.

I woke up rehearsing the dream in my mind; then I took out my journal and wrote it down. I could relate to crevasses and dark places, where caterpillars dwell in trees. I had been in dark places most of my life, until I got the pull and unction; and I wanted a change. The process of going into a secure place of change, was painful. It required dismantling myself and starting over. I was going through a transformative process. I had been very lonely with just me and the kids. I cried many tears and prayed my way through long nights. It was God's word that encouraged and sustained me. Going from who I was to what I was becoming, was a lot of hard work. The last episode in my life had constricted me. I could not move; I could not see. I took note of the words the caterpillar heard, while in the cocoon. Mother of a nation, and a support to your husband. I highlighted the words I wrote about the fingertip beautifying me.

When I got my son home and sat on the couch, I wanted to lose my mind. All the hard work and struggle, then this. What was next. What would

I go through? When was enough, enough… what more Lord! I felt tired, worn out and defeated. I had made it through so much but had anxiety of what more could come. Nothing could rest my mind, I said, “God, I don’t want this anymore… I’m leaving!” I didn’t want to endure anymore. I quit my job. I couldn’t do it anymore. I went from a press- to a crawl, inching my way. I was low in spirits and energy. I told God I was ready for the people to come, wrap me in a straitjacket and take me away.

It was March of 2011, I decided one morning to go to church. I had not been in church since 2006 but something was compelling me. I went to church and the preacher said, “someone told God, you were throwing in the towel, well he told me to tell you; he's throwing it back to you." I went home and cried like a baby. Then I got up, prayed and got my mind back on track. I began to realize my son was always in God's hands, even three days journey away, in Arizona. God always knew that when I sent my son, time would bring him back to me. It was no surprise to God, that my son's dad had moved back to Illinois, it was no surprise to God that my divorce decree was in place. God knew the best way for my son to know and see evil was real; would be to experience it in his hands. I had worried and been full of anxiety and fear. Not realizing or knowing how powerful God was. This experience had stretched my faith. I realized at this point that I did not know the future but no matter what comes my way, God was with me and would always work things out. When God had given me the scripture with Peter. He already knew I was impetuous; he already knew I was being brave in a storm. God also knew I did not have the faith it took to walk on water; to supersede and defy all logic. The incident with my son had shook my very core and rattled me. I sank, I threw in the towel, but God rescued me.

The first thing I needed to do, at this point in my life; was to get in touch with each of the kids. See what they were doing, and where they were at in life. The incident with my son had me totally distracted, but now I was going to catch up on things. My oldest was on her own, and in 2011 she was 21. My oldest son was sixteen, he was a sophomore in school, and staying out of trouble. The twins were thirteen and doing well in school.

My middle child was fourteen, in school but staying in trouble. I fought tooth and nail to keep him out of the streets, even if it meant reporting him missing to the police. The next few years were rough, but nothing compared to the past decade.

In time, both of my sons came to talk to me about things they remembered at their dads. Hidden fears or things they pieced together, the manipulation, the violence and control. Although it didn't work out, I think, it slowed both down. The son I rescued admitted he was doing lots of things he should not be doing and learning way more than he would have learned at home. He was having fun and hadn't asked to come home. He told me it took me coming back for him to realize the mental abuse and control his dad had in his home. My middle son endured and saw a lot, as he matured in age, but somehow when true danger found his crowd, he escaped.

Since I had quit my job; I had to find a new hustle. After me and my son got back home and the van broke down; I had a sensor replaced, and the van was back up. I had no idea what I was going to do for money. Thank goodness I had a little savings. The year I moved into my home, was a qualifying year for a tax bonus, for new homeowners. This was due to the housing crash, that happened shortly before. My income tax I received in 2010, for 2009, was double, what I usually get. Although I had a little stashed away, I had to find a source of income. I drove around town trying to come up with an idea. I passed by a college, they had a big sign that said, now enrolling. I drove up, went inside, and asked if I could speak to somebody about their programs. I had learned, with grants, I could make good money. That day, I was enrolled to get my paralegal studies degree. I had one year, in order to complete. I went to night school and found a job at a daycare, during the day. By summer 2012, I graduated. I couldn't go to my graduation, but I got my diploma in the mail. When I opened it, I saw I had achieved magna cum laude. I had no idea what that meant, or that I had achieved it. When I looked it up it meant, graduating with honors. The moment I read the meaning; I heard a voice. The voice was much like the one in the dream that spoke to the caterpillar, in the cocoon. The voice said, master of the law.

Hearing those words; felt like my first accomplishment. I had worked hard on myself, and I felt, that was my reward. When I was in my early twenties, I used to be so hopeful something would appear before my eyes, although I was never sure what. Now I know hard work with direction and determination; and good things were happening. Dreams come from being deliberate. Good things don't just appear. I had studied God's word; and although I didn't totally grasp it, I tried. I tried to love others, as myself; I put God first, and trusted and believed him. When the word told me, that if I have an ought with my brother, to tell him, I did it. Everything I read I applied, the best way I knew how. Finally, God was speaking. I had tried and tried till I succeeded.

By 2013, my oldest son, came out of school; and was ready to move out. My middle son was still in school and hanging out. The twins were in their sophomore year, and my daughter began cheerleading. My daughter would go on to see things I never imagined for her. She cheered on one of the most elite teams in the nation. By 2016, she had gone to Disneyworld three times and seen a lot of prestige's places. I noticed a difference on her life. I noticed doors that opened for her and ways that were made. I watched as school zones were changed, the year she was going to high school, and school zones were changed back; the year after she graduated. Both twins graduated in 2016. I was so proud. My middle son stayed in school till 2015. In 2013 I had gone back to be a telephone operator, on my old job. I worked for the same company but handled calls for a different outsourcing business. I had lost my way, stumbled, but I was getting on track. I had gone through a time of much pressure, a time that was so dark; I could not see. The kids were growing up. As they grew up and moved away or got in dangers; it tore apart my heart. My heart didn't break, as I lost each of my babies, it tore into pieces. There was a time I had given up on God, but I began to understand. He was doing something through all the pressure, darkness and fatigue. He was changing me.

I understood all the parts of my dream with the bunkers and the storm. I had done well, through tribulation; but everything must be tested and proven. When it came time, would I hand God my son? Would I adhere, when he said give him to me?

Would I trust God, more than I trusted myself? My son's time with his dad, had humbled him. He was no longer the bully, now that he's been bullied. He was no longer the aggressor now that he's endured aggressiveness. He was gentler and more kind. He knew evil existed and as the years went on, he avoided a lot of major downfalls. The storm had proven and tried me. In the dream I was searching for a key, so that after the storm passed, I could leave. The key was my understanding. Understanding that God is! He is all powerful, all knowing, he is God. I understood my son belonged to him. I didn't even hold the patent to my myself. I understood most of the dream, with the caterpillar. The only part I did not grasp was the fingertip beautifying me; nor did I see any evidence of a nation, or any man I would support. I've learned I don't have to wonder and ponder. Eventually the dream would happen and once it did, I could expound it.

Chapter Seven

Becoming

One day while driving, fear and worries, popped up in my head. I pulled my car over and said, “Fear, this is the last time you are going to speak to me. Your days are numbered. Prophecies have been fulfilled, and the time is short that you must suffer; for all the things you have done. If you ever speak to me again, I will start a war of prayer.” I put my car in gear and drove home. The mental aspect of anxiety fled. To conquer the physical anxiety; I learned to take a rest day, every week; to give my body rest. I was tired and stressed. There was a man in the Bible, who outran a chariot. No man can do this, on his own. There is a special anointing, that can come upon a man; that allows him to do supernatural things. I had pressed past poverty, by working diligently; and had supernatural strength, to raise my five kids in the mist of degradation. I had escaped a dark lifestyle, with five people on my back; and once that anointing, that carried me through, subsided, my body felt the exertion.

When I had the dream of the bunker, the same place the water went over my head. I now understood the process; I was to go through. I had endured many waters and then a storm and now I must shake off all that had happened and see what was next in life. Trouble had surrounded my mind, like a swarm of bees. I couldn't even think, a solid thought. For a moment I existed, engulfed in anxiety. I had heard church people say, new levels bring bigger devils. I think they were right. As the swarm, in my mind, cleared, I was regaining my courage and sight. The longer I gave my body, a day of rest, the more it recuperated.

Part 2

I was happy, I had gotten my old job back, but I was burnt out. Sometimes when we prematurely leave a situation, before we get all that was intended; we must go back. I pressed to work every day, with no hope or energy. I kept my mind on the scripture that promised, he would renew your strength. One evening when I fell asleep; the shadow of a man, I often dreamt of, came to me. *I was sitting, in a valley, under a tree. I looked up to see the shadow of a man, and I stood up and walked to him. I got down on my knees and began to praise him. The shadow spoke, "you praise me for all that I provide, you praise me for the miracles and wonders I do; but you have never gotten to know, my character."* When I awoke, I went and got my Bible. I opened my bible and scrolled through the scriptures till I found the one that says, God is love. I continued to scroll and came across a scripture, that spoke of God's mercy and goodness. Lastly, I read of his patience, longsuffering and kindness. I set love, longsuffering, kindness, patience and mercy, at the forefront of my mind. My next goal in life was to know of these things.

When I woke up for work the next day I prayed; "God help me to know you, help me to see these things, a better way." I went to work tired, stressed and wearied. I took sixty calls a day. I dealt with rudeness, ignorance, irate customers and many other things. I began daily to search God for how to respond to these people, as I usually responded in frustration and agitation. These people called in, needing someone who was capable to help them. Although I was physically and emotionally drained; I set my mind to listen. Sometimes, I had to listen to people vent and sometimes I had to hear through their confusion. The more I listened, the more I heard; sometimes I needed to hear the thing the person wasn't saying. For each caller, I made myself familiar with them and found every way, I could possibly help. Helping others became my joy. Setting out to resolve issues, became my reason. I began to realize, that people needed me to be knowledgeable, understanding and patient. I learned not to take their frustration personally, and no matter how they treated me; my goal was to help them.

I began to get it. God saw the conditions of men. He saw that they had no way or solution, but they needed a cure. After some time on the job, it only took me a few minutes on the phone, to know what a person would need. Within a year, there was no question I had not heard and no answer I had not discovered. How much more does God know what we need, how much more does God have all the answers. God is an unselfish, giving, God. He saw the world needed a deliverer and a friend, who could see their needs and offer himself to help them. God gave to people who had nothing to give in return. He had patience with people, who had misdirected outrage, at him. When people didn't get him, he was longsuffering and kind. Every day he had new mercy. I remember I would sit and listen to customers who had previously called. They were angry that no solution had been made for their situation. I knew those other operators were not me and that if they gave me a chance, I would find a remedy. So many people try everything but God. If they just took a moment to let God try, he held all answers and would always be by their sides. No matter how much we struggled, he woke us up again; giving us another day, to get things right. Although God is all powerful and in a position of authority, he was humble, meek and kind. God is the creator, yet he doesn't prance. He sits, waits and hopes, for the day we decide to know him. God is peaceful, he isn't a hell raising God, full of contention. Amid adversity and turmoil, God can bring joy. God was gentle, no matter how many times I didn't understand; he devised a way to teach me. The more I understood the character of God, the more I wanted to be like him. The more I worked to be like him, the more the content of my talks- changed. I became in awe, with a God so mighty and powerful; who can work wonders and miracles; yet was so humble and meek.

I began to realize; God had a solution for me. He always knew that all my prayers, would be resolved, but not in an instant and not in a day. I saw that when I prayed for my change; it was much like making a cake. God heard me and he began to mix in the ingredients, with the right measure. He prepared the perfect fire and put me in it. He always maintained the perfect atmosphere, so that I could rise and be firm. He watched and when everything came together, he took me out. I learned that everything doesn't happen in an instant, and depending on what we pray, we must trust the master's way, of giving it.

2013 through 2016, was a time of being still. I remained still while the fingertip of God beautified me. Wonders, miracles and power; are awesome, but the most wonderful thing to encounter is love. One of the greatest rewards, we have daily, is God's mercy. I am thankful for religion; religion taught me, Jesus Christ. All the things Jesus did, had a purpose. The purpose was for us to learn, through religion, the steps to be delivered, enlightened, healed, and cleansed. Once we understood the mission of Jesus Christ, we were led by his spirit, into relationship, with God. God fellowships and recognizes, his own. When we are envious and full of malice and hate, we are as foreigners to God; but when we clothe ourselves, in God's attributes; we have the makeup, to become sons and daughters. God not only wanted to deliver me, clean me up and make me new. He wanted relationship. He wanted me to know him personally, through spiritual intimacy.

God began to show me, through my dreams, that I must get rid of all my baggage; to move on in him. God had great places for me to go, but my resentments, anger, disappointments; couldn't go. All the people, that ever wronged or hurt me, I forgave. We have all hurt someone, so I had no high horse, to be on. To all the people, that looked past me, in my worst state; that's okay, God does wonders, by his mite, alone. To all the people, that rejected me, that was part of God's plan. I could not harbor, anything. All my dirty laundry could not come with me, where I was going.

The more I interacted at work, with customers, the more discernment and insight I began to have; to see the important things in matters. I developed empathy and once in touch with who they were; I understood what was important to them and how they wanted to be treated. It is hard to explain my insight, so I wrote this essay to try and describe it.

ANTIQUITY

Discernment is a great tool to have in, seeing people. To see them is to understand their

needs. Taking what is seen with the eyes and heard with the ears and allowing a perception to manifest. A perception of the things, we cannot see; the things in the person's heart, mind and character that develop the atmosphere surrounding them. Once you've learned truth and honesty; you recognize it, when you hear it. You begin to learn confusion, frustration and deception. You may pick up on agenda, but the agenda is not significant.

If we could see this atmosphere, it would be best interpreted; using colors and representations, so that the mind can grasp the perception. It is not always easy, to transfer, unseen ideas into tangible depictions; but if one searches the information, once they are

enlightened, they can begin to see the facts. Much like people being told, in the air, there are vapors; there is no way to see this, but once enlightened they can begin to search for proofs. In school, kids are told; there are vapors all around them. To prove this, they are shown two cups. You fill one cup, or the first cup, halfway-with water, marking the water level. You place a second cup, on top of the first; and over time, continue to use a marker, to mark the water levels. Over time you will see the water level drops in the first cup and droplets appear in the top cup. Using shaving crème and dye, the water in the top cup will eventually form a cloud, thereby proving your theory of the unseen. The water is transferred from one cup to the other,

although the transference, is not visible to the eyes; but the two cups hold the proof.

Humans emit things, into the atmosphere, that transform not into clouds, but into elevation. Not elevation, into the sky, but elevation in life. This elevation is not limited to positions or rank, but also tranquility, peace and inner happiness. You will run across people whose actions and words will depict anger, vexation, frustration, greed, or jealousy, or peace, joy, contentment, or warmth. These things radiate into things I will attempt to paint for our minds. The proof of these things will be evident in the soot or residue seen in that person's life; or everything surrounding them, or that they touch. Of course, all the experiments and

investigative work I will leave to you, your life being the best-case study. Your actions and attitudes, or things you see, will transform into, the things manifested in your life. I will use colors to depict the atmospheres.

The first color observed is black. Black is symbolic of a void, a complete emptying out, futility. Black tends to draw a certain aloneness; it can almost be described as engulfing versus radiating. The wonderful thing about black, is within it, are all colors. Black is neither happy nor sad, it is almost a resting place, between realms. It has in it, the ability to burst into anything, it decides to become. The main characteristic that forms from black, is a person

who's quiet and at peace in one cup, whose atmosphere produces a life at rest.

Grey is sullen, it emits a certain sadness and draws unproductive things. It is alive but fruitless, ungiving, inept. Grey tends to draw grey, has a heavy energy and is much life looking at a book, full of pictures of the Sahara Desert. Greys tend to generate a mundane life with a lot of hype and vain words on the other side.

Yellow is warm and inviting. If I could give yellow a face, it would be that of Marry Poppins. An eminence of unlimited possibilities, the mind of a complete Pollyanna. There is no mountain too high, no valley too low; just put on a smile and be determined to climb; believing fun, laughter, and experience will be gained

along the way. Once people come across this atmosphere, they tend to follow it, because the experience of it; allows their space to feel warm. On the other side of this atmosphere, is accomplishment after accomplishment.

My final color is white, but understand, there are plenty of colors between the ones I have mentioned. White is a strong aurora. One, that many people don't approach, but squirrels and butterflies would enjoy basking in. One I would liken to the perception of mother nature; people are in awe but dare not get too close or incite. White is where black can go to be ignited or from where yellow developed their laughter. A color of power and no nonsense; a color of authority. The character of this color is one that

thrives on knowledge and exhibits much wisdom, on the other side or in the second cup; you will find someone completely and totally blessed.

Although these colors cannot be seen with the eye, there are proofs of them. There are many colors to be discovered. Colors are the best way I had to paint a picture for the mind. The reasoning is done from the things you can see and hear- to the things that become from them. I've only painted a picture of the invisible thing linking them.

Life is designed, that when you do facetious or dark things; there are weights applied. Some people may call it karma. It is much harder to stay above water, while carrying weights. The more weights you have, the harder it is; for you to succeed or flourish. A lot of people, that do dark works, tend to spread soot to all they touch. It's the same token as misery loves company. If they are miserable, they will make others miserable, around them. Jealous and envious people tend to be very unhappy; and if you hang around them for long, you will be too. I have always taken note, that people who are always giving, always have something to give, whereas stingy people, are always asking. The more I changed my attitudes and character; the more I saw changes, in my surroundings and life. I no longer attracted the same kind of people. Most people I used to attract, no longer wanted to be around me. The kinder and more considerate I became, the more favor I noticed. As I changed, so did my atmospheres and as my

atmospheres changed so did the evidence in my life.

Not only had my character and life changed; God had taken my abilities and duplicated them in a spiritual way. We are not only carnal. Our flesh is only a house for the true thing that matters. Although the spirit cannot be seen with the eyes; once it is awakened, it has senses. The same way our bodies must be fed; our spirit must be fed. We eat natural things for substance, we feed our spirit man with word. If you eat pork chops and cake every day; your body reflects it. If you feed your mind a bunch of junk, your spirit man reflects it. All spiritual things are shown through natural things, or creation. Just like our bodies have DNA, our spirit has DNA. Spiritual DNA tells who you are through your attributes, or character. When God sees his DNA, in you, he calls you son or daughter. Our bodies have need of water, our spirit has need of God. Man has many states or forms. Just like ice, we see ourselves in solidity. We also have a spirit, whose works are manifest, in the things we do; and when we leave here, we will leave as a vapor, to be collected somewhere else. Water is not God's greatest creation; man is and how much more complex are we than it. I had various skill sets. One of my strongest skills is reasoning. I loved geometry. Proving facts and theorems. God took my skills and created gifts. My ability to grasp allowed me to see things that did not line up with Gods word. Things men had created and began to call the church but did not prove once illuminated by the word.

I was beginning to see life in a parallel realm. Things weren't so simple to me, as black and white. I was ready to set sail, and soar. I had vision, like an eagle; I had received my change. I not only had natural senses; I now had spiritual senses. Wisdom(eyes), knowledge(ears), empathy(touch), discernment(smell), and experience(taste)… having all five allowed me to grasp.

Chapter Eight

Ashton

It was mid-summer, 2016. My youngest daughter came to me and told me; she was pregnant. I didn't have a lot of thoughts on the matter, I just took it in. Come fall of 2016, my daughter came to me and sat on my bed. She sat there for hours, then finally; in the middle of the night, she began to speak. She told me she had two dreams. In one dream the doctors came and took her baby and she never saw the baby again. In the second dream the doctors told her the baby was going to die. I listened to her, tell her dreams; without commenting or making expressions. I had seen that my daughter, had a special call on her life; now I knew she was a dreamer. I learned to heed dreams. I knew her ultrasound was the next day. She had told me she didn't want me to go to the ultrasound, because she wanted to have a gender reveal; she felt I wouldn't be able to keep the information to myself. Although I was concerned, after she told her dreams; I followed her wish and I did not go. The next day at work; I was on my first break and saw that I had a missed call, from my youngest daughter. I called her back and she was crying. She said, "mom they are telling me my baby won't make it." I told her I would be right there, and I left work.

When I reached the doctor's office; I asked them to explain to me what was going on. My daughter was discombobulated, so I encouraged her that there is nothing God cannot do, and everything is up to him. The specialists and doctors came in and pulled up the ultrasound. They began to show me the baby's development and told me they believe he has a symptom, they term, incompatible with life. The actual name of the condition, they quoted that day, I didn't commit to memory. The condition was not the death sentence. A symptom of the condition is why they felt the baby wouldn't live. The doctors and specialists gave up right there, but my daughter wanted to know more. An amniocentesis was scheduled. At the amniocentesis, I tried to be close to her. I comforted her and rubbed her head, and when they showed her the needle, I took her hand. The doctor explained the process. She explained, they would stick the needle through her stomach, her uterus and into the amino sack. When the doctor was ready, my daughter pushed my hand away. I was dumbfounded. She was everyone's baby. Everyone coddled her and here she was being so brave.

The doctor took some fluids and explained they would be sent to the lab; to determine or prove the condition, they felt the baby had. Sometime later, we went in for the results. They explained the baby didn't have what they thought, but he had duplicated 7p22. They explained that the baby's seventh chromosome had an extra piece on one of the rods. This would cause the chromosomes to make irregular patterns, causing deformities. The doctor came close to my daughter, sat down and took her hand. She looked in my daughters' eyes and said, "there is something we don't understand. We found that you have the same condition." The doctor explained that it didn't make sense and wanted to ask my daughter some questions. They asked if she was delayed or had any learning disabilities. My daughter explained, she was not delayed and didn't have any learning disabilities. After they finished talking, I asked the doctor if my daughter is a miracle? The doctor responded, "this is the first case we have ever seen in our lab; we can't explain how your daughter is here, so yes, she may be."

Knowing that she had the condition, made her determined, to not give up on her baby. My daughter did her research and found one of the best, if not the best, children's hospitals. She made an appointment to go there, for her baby. Before we went to the children's hospital, they did an echo and found the baby had problems with his heart. We were not concerned with the heart because the first step was understanding the symptom, they said would kill him. The baby had an encephalocele. When the chromosomes were replicating, it caused deformities. The only life-threatening deformity caused the encephalocele.

The hospital was in another state, an hour away. I didn't have the money for gas or a hotel. We borrowed what we could and decided we would drive down, drive back; and drive back down, the next day for the results. We got to the hospital; I was so impressed. Parents and babies were everywhere. I watched the families and overheard some, who were there for their children's hearts. I didn't say anything, but I smiled and thought how blessed they are. The hospital did a large test called an MRI, that looked at the entire body through different angles. The next day we went back and sat in a huge room; filled with every type of specialist you can imagine. We sat and listened as each specialist explained the different parts of the baby's body. They explained his skull last. Up till then, I still had hope. They explained when the skull formed it left a minuscule crack. The crack let in spinal fluid which damaged his brain. They showed the areas of brain damage, then explained what they were seeing, that concerned them. The baby wasn't swallowing, they could tell, because babies swallow the amino fluids; but my daughter had an overwhelming amount of fluid.

This meant that there was damage to the brain stem. The brain stem tells the body to breath.

When I heard this, my head fell, and I silently cried. My attention immediately moved to my baby. I asked if she could deliver here. They said she could. She immediately said no; I want everyone at home to meet him. I didn't feel comfortable with her delivering at home, because the doctors seemed so crude about him and didn't have as much knowledge. I told them that the doctor at home wants her to deliver the baby vaginally. One of the doctors sat up, looked concerned and said. "We have found that in these cases, the encephalocele gets stuck. The baby is breach, so what normally happens, is the head will get stuck and the baby will hang there, possibly for hours."

I told the panel of doctors, the doctors back home told my daughter, the baby would never live.

A doctor spoke up and said no one knows but God. So, we went home understanding that our little baby, more than likely would die, or live a rough life. The doctors had also explained that some people would rush the baby to surgery in hopes of saving the babies life. They advised against this, as most of the time, the baby would die alone, being cut on.

It was the second week in December and the baby was due at the end of January. I began to pray for my daughter's safety, as what she would endure, was dangerous. I also told God that I would love to hear, my grandson's voice. While praying I remembered a sermon God had placed in my spirit, a couple of years before. The sermon was, "what if the answer is no?" I couldn't explain why God was sending for my grandson. Despite his body my grandson was a soul. I always focused more on what he was going through than what we were going through. He was all that mattered -getting him through this transition. It was January 2nd and for one reason or another, I missed work and stayed at home. I woke up to, “Mom!” I immediately became afraid that I would go to my daughter and see a baby coming out. She shouted again, and I got up. When I got to the hallway, she was standing there, water was everywhere. I said get dressed. I called all her siblings and told them to meet us at the hospital; then I got my daughter in the car.

When we got to the hospital. They took my daughter to get prepped and the surgeons got ready. The doctors were so careful; they moved slowly, because sudden movement could shift the waters in his brain and kill him. I sat there and talked to my daughter, while she was lying on the table. After ten to fifteen minutes, they had him out. While cleaning him, they poured a blue liquid in his mouth; then wrapped him and laid him on her chest. I talked to him and I have recordings, I can swear he spoke back. His cry was faint, and he smiled when he heard his mother's voice. We spent thirteen hours with him, then his breathing became faint. I remembered reading that God spread the sunrise. God came by to get him at 5:55AM, on January 2, 2017. We thank God for the time we had. He meant so much in such a short time.

At the funeral, the preacher used Ashton's story to encourage everyone, especially young people. She told them, that like Ashton's, their lives matter. She encouraged them to fight for their lives as Ashley had fought for her sons. My daughter had shown more love and been more protective of her baby, in those months; than I had been in her eighteen years. Ashton's short life had purpose. He taught his mom; she was more of a warrior than she would have ever imagined. He touched his uncles, in a profound way and caused them to rethink how they see life. He brought me and my daughter closer than two friends. He taught us that no one knows the mind of God and to never second guess him. We learned to appreciate thirteen hours rather than complain about his short life. Through his experience, we learned Ashley was a possible miracle, and there was a purpose to her life.

We do not know why God allowed us all, to experience this. One day, about a year later; me and my youngest daughter, went to church. The woman preaching talked about broken homes and children who had to suffer, because their parents didn't want to be parents. The preacher talked about the struggle for the child to overcome and to heal from hurt. Then the preacher said this generational cycle, ends right here. Me and Ashley cried, knowing my father had left, her father had left, and Ashton's wasn't' there. I don't' know the mind of God. I believe Ashton got a golden ticket, into eternity. Much like every baby that leaves prematurely. In eternity he would receive good. I was sad that he had to taste death. He had to endure the hardest struggle of life before all of us. I felt for my daughter, as she had to grapple to understand. Losing a baby is a huge loss, full of disappointment. I rarely saw my daughter cry, although her head was bowed down. Within months my daughter had signed up for job training. She would be going away.

I believe with all my heart that Ashton was not alone. There was a night I slept in my daughters' room, with her. I had a bad hip, that had felt out of place for months. The night I slept in her room I heard sounds. I heard plainly, my middle sons' soul, calling for me. That night my hip was popped back in place. I believe angels ministered to my grandson. I don't believe for a minute, that he suffered alone.

The experience with Ashton showed me how much I had prevailed in God. It was like a butterfly seeing its reflection for the first time. I had become a mother and a leader and a granny. I had become the matriarch of my family. I learned to be a support and a silent friend. I remember one time, I went to see a man that was dying, to say goodbye. I walked in his room and the first thing I asked was how are you doing. I could have kicked myself for my foolishness. Now through this experience I know exactly what to say. Going through a loss of a loved one; grows us in many ways.

Chapter Nine

Butterfly

I can imagine, through my experience, that when a butterfly evolves; there is confusion on who they are and where they should be. I began to relate, to one of my favorite television characters. There was a television show that came on when I was young. In the show, a man received a visit from another world. They left him with a superhero suit and a book of instructions on how to use it. Unfortunately, he lost the book and had to struggle on how to use his powers. I felt like that man. I had been endowed with special gifts. I began to see who I was in life; and I had evolved spiritually, as well. It took a lot of courage to step out and be what I had never been. I had often sat in church and wondered

why I didn't fit. Once I understood, I wrote this

- ❖ One day, Grasshopper, Ladybug, Ant, Worm, Snail and Butter, were all sitting under the tree.
- ❖ Ladybug said, "guess what, I'm getting married, I'm now going to be First Ladybug.
- ❖ Grasshopper said, "I'm so full of hope, pastor called me Grass the Hoper.
- ❖ Ant said, "I'm so busy I'm now Worker Ant, full of helps.
- ❖ Worm said, "I'm so faithful, they're going to call me Willing Worm."
- ❖ Snail says, "I've performed such works they're going to call me Deacon Snail.
- ❖ Everyone began to wonder, what about Butter?
- ❖ The next season under the tree came: Grass the Hoper, First Ladybug, Worker Ant, Willing Worm and Deacon Snail.
- ❖ Ant looked around and said, "where is Butter?"
- ❖ They all looked puzzled and began to discuss where Butter may be.
- ❖ Ant looked up and said, "look, everybody, up there…
- ❖ Butter can fly."

Around 2005, right before the church collapsed, I had a dream. During that time, I was the dishwasher. I sat in church and watched, couple after couple, get married. I remained positive in my time of hurt and wanted to find something I could do. I placed myself in a position; nobody had, and nobody would want. A position, washing dishes. One night during this time, I dreamt. *In the dream, I was at a symphony. I stood behind the curtains with a mop and bucket, waiting to do my job. Right before the show started, a man came to me. He took my mop, and handed me a wand; then said, "direct." The curtains opened and there, before a large audience and a symphony, I stood.* God took the lowliest and poorest, member; and made them into what he had declared she would always be. Just like a caterpillar was always a butterfly.

I knew who I had become in God. I do not like titles, but I can explain the works. I had gotten to a stature where I was placed to direct. I read something once that said, "when you are seated at a table you don't have to situate yourself at the head; because when you are gifted the table will shift." Author unknown. God showed me he had loosed my tongue and he told me to speak. It does not matter who likes or does not like, what is being said, if what is being said comes with the highest authority or backing. All the gifts I mentioned that allowed me to grasp would be needed to speak, because God cannot back anything outside of himself.

Chapter Ten

Revealing

May of 2017, my operator job was ending. The company that was outsourcing, to my company, no longer needed our services. Some of the workers found other jobs, for our company; and a few of us took a separation package. I received a month of pay and two months of unemployment. Enduring paid off. I had been so tired and burned out, but I held on, believing there was more on that job; God was trying to do in me.

My youngest daughter would be an hour away, at the training program, until December of 2017. My youngest son was working, and leading praise service at his church. My middle son was working and trying life out on his own. My oldest son had purchased his first car, a Lexus; he was working hard and had his own place. My oldest daughter was working hard, and in her own place as well.

I was relaxing and beginning to wonder, what I would do now. For so long, I had given my whole heart, to be a mother. Now I was faced with me. I had plenty of time on my hands, to rest and reflect. After a week of being off work, I sat down in front of the computer to find a job. It was nice, not being in a press to find a job. I was taking my time and figuring out what I wanted to do. I hated being locked down, in a dim lit cubicle, for hours. I gave thought and decided to apply as a bus monitor, for the public schools. I got the job and would start training in June. I would have a full-time position to begin work in August. While online, applying for the job; my curiosity led me to the web page, for the University I attended as a teen. The university was in my hometown of Lexington and had one of the winningest basketball teams.

I started training for my new job, in the beginning of June; and continued to wait on a response from the University. By mid-June, I received a letter, letting me know, I would have to go through a panel; to request admission back into the college. I followed all the instructions of the letter, prepared and found all the needed documents; then scheduled an interview date. The interview went well, and the panel approved me, for admission. I went home and began my financial aid process. I learned that I had used all my grant money but would qualify for loans. Loans wouldn't be enough to cover tuition and books. I got a little down and walked into my room. My eyes were drawn to a letter on my dresser. I picked up the envelope and read the contents inside. The program that built my home, offered scholarships. I had laid the letter on my dresser because I was curious to what it was; but I had forgotten, to open it. I was excited but not surprised.

I applied for the scholarship and was approved. The scholarship would be paying my tuition. The job, I would be starting, had a split shift. I worked three hours in the early morning; taking the kids to school, then I was off five hours till I returned, to pick the kids up. I got online to schedule my classes, but found it almost impossible to line up majors, classes I would need, and opportunity to take them; being I couldn't arrive till ten. I made an appointment to see an academic advisor. My advisor was extremely knowledgeable and happened to be the chair, on the panel, that allowed me to come back to school. She listened to my situation, looked at my transferred classes and classes I had taken there, previously.

After doing all the math, she took off her glasses and looked up at me. She told me that there was a program that had started the previous semester for people like me. It was a new program, that offered a Bachelor of Liberal Studies. It is designed to give leniency to the type of classes needed, allowing a plethora to work with, for scheduling. My advisor made all the changes in the system, to declare my major, designed a roadmap to finishing, and a first semester schedule.

Doors were opened for me to go back to a university, I had once failed. The scholarship I had lost, would be replaced. A program was designed, not even a year prior, for people like me with hectic schedules. God was returning to me the years I had lost. He allowed me to suffer and go through as that little girl knowing that once all hell came against me, and Satan took his blow, that he could restore.

I started my new job, and college in August 2017. By May of 2019 I was walking with my Bachelor. I had an inkling, but wasn't sure, what this degree would do for me. I had heard what God said, but had no clue, to the road that would get me there. In 2019, my youngest daughter was working harder than I ever had, she had her own place, and was driving a vehicle nicer than mine. She had a few stumbles, dealing with the loss of her son. His first birthday was extremely hard. My youngest son had one foot in, and one foot out, but that was okay. He was only twenty-one, so he had a little more time to get his vision straight.

I had decorated my living room; it was as beautiful as my dad had decorated ours, when I was a child. My youngest son had painted all my rooms, over the past couple of years; and by the time he had finished, his skills looked professional. I took one of the kid's old bedrooms, cleared it out and made it an office. I took another room and made it a den. I began growing plants, I loved to watch them grow, and I loved their beauty. I bought a sewing machine. I had gone as far as taking it out of the box. Life was good. My job only paid for 183 days out of the year, but it was enough to pay bills, food, gas and spending. I had traded in the van and gotten a convertible, but that was paid off.

I had enough time on my hands, so I took time to write a book. I learned how to be a thorough editor. I had always loved graphic design; it was therapeutic to design covers. I have always loved to write, and in college I learned tools, for better writing. Bachelor of Liberal Studies is a great diploma for a career in publishing. I learned all the steps to publishing, and I grew in my writing the more I edited. As I was compiling this book; I wrote three kid's books and began to promote them to the school system I work for.

I had embraced my place in God, and I had achieved everything I could have ever thought to achieve; but there were things unresolved in me. I could pretend to be so strong but a part of me was empty. I was biding my time, but I was not living. There was a time in my life that I had the biggest dreams. One of the most powerful things about me were my hopes. My hopes had propelled me to be unstoppable. There were many times I would hear God say breathe. I tried to hope but it was as if I had forgotten how. A part of me ached. I had searched for a mate, but it seemed one could not be found. I had tried, I had believed, I had waited; but no one came. The supernatural strength that was close to me, seemed to be gone. I was not in a Tribulus hell anymore, therefore I did not need that powerful strength that made me laugh in the worst of times. It was like living life as only Clark Kent. During tribulation, God was not only my best friend; he was my comrade. He had been with me in the war, he had been my everything, when I had nothing. Now that life was normal, I did not know what to do. I was sitting on the sidelines waiting on the one I adored. Then one morning, I had the hope to believe the ominous power was still there and he will hear me if I speak. I set my mind to hope again. I had to get back to being intentional and making things happen; rather than wondering why certain things, like marriage, had never happened for me.

I had spent a lot of time enduring, but the turmoil was over, and I had to find my wings to live.

Chapter eleven

Full Fruition

The path I had walked came with a lot of abandonment and rejection, which comes with the territory. Life seemed to have hardened me. I was resilient but had become impenetrable. For the next phase of life God had to soften me and it began with a dream. *In the dream I was in a place that had the appearance of a hospital. The place was large with white floors and appeared sterile. I got onto an elevator and the doors closed. Instead of going up, the elevator opened on the other side and I walked through. I then saw the path I had taken that led me to a house. I walked around the house into the back yard and saw three forms, of men. Two of the men were digging a hole, and the third form was bound and lying on the ground. I became afraid. I ran into the house and dialed 911. The voice of a man answered and said, "I know what they are doing, leave them alone."* I woke up got my journal and began to write and as I wrote I gained understanding. The place I had been was in a realm of prayer. I had been praying amongst a group of people with a fervent faithful prayer life and it had allowed me to be in a pure clean atmosphere that drenched me in healing. This was the place I saw that was like a hospital that allowed me to pass through into another place or atmosphere. Once my soul had been drenched, I could be set free of something I didn't even know had been with me. Some things are so entangled and deep rooted in our spirits that we need spiritual surgery to remove them.

When I saw the figure, in the dream, bound in the back yard; I had become afraid because the figure is something I had identified with all of my life, but the voice on the phone knew what was going on and wanted me to be still and allow the process. The two figures were digging a hole for the spirit of rejection. They would bury it and it would not bother me ever again. Rejection is a horrible spirit likened to a watery puss filled sore, that spreads infection throughout everything it is upon. Once I had been cleansed of it, it had to be buried. Everything I had been through had left me hardened. After that dream, I realized how rough around the edges I was. A waiter could ask me if I wanted separate checks, and I would look at him crazy, wondering if he asked because I look poor. I had to realize; I was no longer in a war. I had to see that seasons change; the rough process a diamond goes through, does not always last. I had defied odds, I had fought through poverty; and because of all the battles, my face carried a stern look. God made use of the resilience that I had determined I must have as a child, to get me through all the darkness. Now that I had made it through, I softened my heart, then softened my face. Not everyone comes to hurt you or oppress you. I learned to trust that God had me; he was my protector and my defender. I didn't have to fight anymore. I learned to love me and do sweet things for me. I learned being a girl, doesn't mean I am weak; and showing need, doesn't mean I'm not strong. I wanted to be vulnerable, love, give and receive. God showed me that the same wall I had put up to keep from being hurt, is the same wall that will keep me from being loved. A huge wound is obtained when you feel you were not worthy of your own mothers' acceptance and love. Yes, my life had been rough, and yes, I had been alone and destitute; but seasons change. I had to stop living in what was and start living what was going to be.

One of the last dreams I had. *I was sitting in my house, with a smile on my face. I was full and satisfied, when the shadow of a man came to me. He sat beside me and held my hand. He said, "there's one last thing we have to do; come with me." I walked with him, and mysteriously, we came to a room. He said, "go in." I went in and I heard a girl crying. I walked to the closet and opened the door. I saw the little girl I had left behind, sitting there, still waiting for me. I bent my knees and got close to her, then gave her a hug. I said, "everything is alright now, you can come out." I turned around to see the shadow of a man behind me. I stood there and he spoke. "When you thought you were alone, you weren't." "I never left you, I was the light in the closet." "When a mother or father forsakes, then, I rear up." "She was never by herself, but great things aren't made in easy ways." "When evil things come to people. I don't always remove the evil. Sometimes I incorporate myself in the situation; and in time the person will see, that with me, they are stronger than they think."*

It is now the fall of 2020. I have been home from work because of a pandemic. At this point I have been single for over twenty years. I have had a lot of time to search out, study and watch what was important to ascertaining love; so, I wrote a book GREEN BEANS AND CANDY BARS, A GUIDEBOOK TO LOVE AND LUST. Here at this juncture I feel complete, but God has been dealing with me. He began to deal with me about my house. I had become everything I was birthed to be, everything that was hidden in my DNA. Author, teacher, scholar, entrepreneur, mom; but God was showing me that he was going to take the house I built and adorn it. He showed me how he can take who I am or my set of circumstances and change it as simply as I can take a bedroom, fill it with a couch loveseat and television and it becomes a den. Many times, while sitting quietly, I have heard God speak to me. "When your husband left, you trusted me. That part of you that has been crippled for generations I am going to fix. No longer will you be barren in a place where your family has been barren, for generations. No longer will children be fatherless. I have changed the curse of dysfunction and abuse. You are the matriarch of something new. The protégé whose lineage is of greater." My mind immediately thought of how old I am. And God responded to my thoughts, "that doesn't change anything." When I thought of the words I had heard in my dream, mother of a nation. I was looking and wondering what people this is whom I would become their mother. In what way would I be a mother to them. Then I realized, it was not a people I would be over but a lineage and legacy that would come out of me.

From the beginning God established a pattern. Kids were never meant to be unprotected;

families were never meant to be split up. All the changes we have made has wrought carnage and desolation. Family is important, family is a design by God; and God was going to restore it to my lineage. For years I continued to see a pattern. Every time I glanced at a clock it was 4:44. I began to realize this was not coincidental. God situates things in patterns. Families are a pattern of life, and a component for this thing to be, would be situated in me understanding matrimonial love.

Chapter twelve

Green Beans and Candy Bars

As I was approaching the age of fifty, I had a startling revelation about myself and men. The only real experiences I had had was in my youth, along with a few encounters in my forties. The man I was currently dating I had met in November of 2017. He had appeared nineteen years to the month, after my husband had left. Although I had aged in years, I had not aged in dating experience. So, I was going in to knowing him with limitations. I soon recognized that he did not respond to me the same, as men I had previously dated. I set out to understand why this man was not impetuous and did not have crazy desires. He did not jump when I snapped, and he did not beg when I threatened to leave. On another note he did things for me, no other man had ever done. So, I set out on a voyage of discovery, to see why.

I began to grapple with an analogy. *There are two men. The first man found a house that he wanted. He loved the house, for everything it had. Hot tub, gazebo, weight room. He was in love! The house had everything he could enjoy. The second man found a house. He loved its stability. He saw the house as something he could build onto and make it into a home. He loved where the house was situated and its vintage appeal. One man had strong emotions about what he wanted and what it would bring to him. The second man had a vision, of what the house had that he could work with to make a home.* When I met my husband in my youth; I had a government apartment and a government check, to offer him. He was pleased to come in, sit like a fat rat and enjoy the freedom of all I had to give. The guy I had recently met, had his own things; and I would soon learn he would have expectations and requirements I had not experienced with men in my past.

I began to realize that the new guy in my life saw me more like the house that had stability. He saw things in me, I had not seen in myself. He valued things about me other men never had. He once remarked that I was the smartest girl he had ever met. I was not used to a man that saw beyond my physical looks. This guy mowed my lawn and was always finding ways to incorporate himself into my life. He let me know he loved spending time with me and treated me very nice. I loved that he could fix anything, from a car to a kitchen sink. I was alone and had never had a man to help me. I appreciated him and looked up to him. The most amazing thing is that he knew how to respond to my crazy. I loved that he did not get crazy in return. He remained poised and spoke to me rather than acting out with me. I was a strong woman, but I did not scare or intimidate him.

Men I dated in the past, brought nothing to the table. They seemed to always love what I had whether physical or accumulated goods. They would melt with my smile but had nothing to offer my mind. I had dated men that loved the house for what it offered, but now I was dating someone who valued me. He often remarked that he loved that I was a nerd. Other men had always tried to get my nerd out of me. They wanted me to be hipper, they wanted me to fit in. The new guy valued my mind and my determination. He commented on how hard I worked and often told me he was proud of me. I noticed little things he saw in me, he implemented into his life. He talked to me about the business he was running and listened when I had ideas.

The change this man brought was refreshing. I was thoroughly intrigued. As I got to know him, I had new questions to ask other men. It was hard for me to give any energy to men who only focused on saying the right things or acting the right way. I was done listening to men who sounded arrogant while thinking I would find their behaviors cute.

I had been at the bottom of the barrel but climbed out and was headed to the top. So, when men met me a lot of things, they had to say would put me off. I was for the underdog. I had compassion for the little man. I did not think I was better than anybody. A lot of men wanted us to be facades together, but the new guy was not like that. He was real and sincere.

I noticed how men treated their kids. How involved they were, how much they thought of them or how distant and detached. I learned that facing our responsibilities were the building blocks to life. Facing the responsibility of being a mom put me in position to lead five adults. Knowing how to take care of my kids put me in position to help with my grandkids. When men wanted to talk to me but could not handle their responsibilities then that is a no-no. There are missing components to their life. In those responsibilities was their potential. If you can so easily put your kids to the side, it would not be that hard for you to do the same with me.

I noticed how this new guy loved his mother. He was very sweet to her and anything she or her sisters needed he was there. Someone had raised a very decent man. I found I no longer wanted projects. Men who were wounded and hurt and took it out on the world. I always wanted to fix it and make them better. This guy was no project, he had a lot of his stuff together. Wanting to be in a relationship to fix somebody is not a healthy way to think. Wanting to be in a relationship to grow to new levels is a great opportunity and for the first time in my life that opportunity was standing in front of me.

Meeting someone different caused me to lose interest in other men. Other men had never stimulated me in ways that he had. This man was able to stimulate my mind. He was able to discuss and give feedback on the biggest parts of my life, and he always showed an interest in me. Other men had always shown an interest in 'it'. Other men were willing to jump through hoops to spend a little time. I had an effect on other men. An effect that seemed to make them beg and sometimes cry. An effect that allowed me to get away with being rude to them and selfish; and yet they still stayed. I could snap and they would jump.

I was great at grabbing other men's attention; but this new guy made me realize that the attention I got from other men was for the moment or in certain moments. Other men would do anything from spending hours on the phone to letting me meet their mothers, but they never became part of my life. This guy valued his time and would rather spend his time making a future than being on the phone. Other men did not take an interest in who I was becoming, or what I was working towards.

The biggest thing I realized, is these other men had nothing on their minds, of any interest to me. They had nothing in their lives that I admired or wanted. Most men could not answer simple questions with responses I could understand. Other men never had questions to ask of me; but this new guy asked me questions that made me think. His questions were so deep that they tapped into my emotions. Emotions that time had caused me to forget. He dug in and wanted to know my hopes, desires and expectations.

The one aspect of this new guy I did not like, at first; is that he did not respond, the way I wanted, to my demands. He did not come running when I had little fits. He did not let me run the show. The more he resisted, the more I became a brat. Boys have no problem with letting women pay the bills and dictate how things would be; but when you meet a man that knows how to pay his own bills, you learn real fast that you won't be running everything.

This man knew how to lead, he did not need me directing him around like a puppy. Telling him where to go, what to do and what I expected. For a while I fought against this new chemistry. Did he not see my sexuality, was he not afraid of what I might do. I would threaten to leave or threaten to be with someone else. Still he remained firm and stood his ground. I pulled out my biggest guns, sexy clothes and offers of fun. That did not sway him. He was truly a commander and chief. I did not understand, so I began to yell. That did not work; so, I called him names, but he did not fight back. He softly told me, not to talk to him like that.

I did not understand, and my mind reached a tizzy. I had never gotten this response from any man I had dated. I was used to ruling a man with sexuality. I was used to having my way. With the new guy something had changed. I pressed beyond threats and went on a couple of dates; realizing, it only made me miss him. I was constantly comparing them to him. I had already made a list of positives and negatives, and knew this new guy was unique and worth it; but I found myself back out in the piranha pool just trying to make a point or get my way.

When I said jump, he acted as if I had not spoken. Hold on, stop the bus! That is not how I expected things to be done. So, one day he shut down. He called it a time out. I did not like it at all. I fussed, I fumed but those actions did not change anything. I made up my mind and became resolute. I would figure out what I needed to do. All the wondering had gotten me nowhere so far, so I turned off my spinning wheel and made a simple decree. Although I did not know what it was, this man had a different reaction towards me. At this point I did not create a label and I did not blame. I simply made a declaration that this man was not the same.

The last thing the new guy told me before I went into time out was that when I see something in the field that is black and white. I have to quit assuming it is a skunk. Every man is not a skunk and if you took the time you may see my character is more like a puppy dog. He was right. I had treated him just like all the other men, without considering that he was not the same.

After fighting, creating petty games, threatening, demanding, and whining; I decided to hear what he was saying. Although something new had presented itself to me, I possessed an old attitude. This man was different, but I was using the reasoning and behaviors that had kept the other kind of men.

I began working on myself. Changing my attitudes and responses. I became kind and learned not to react. I was less stringent and learned to give. I started verbalizing that I appreciated all the things he did, rather than pouting that I did not have more. For at least a year I acted right. I followed his lead, and I did not start fights. I watched and I waited while learning a different way, and eventually I mellowed. I even became a little sweet.

In time I valued even more things in him. A man that encouraged me to improve my character and have a heart that learned to give. I moved beyond liking him, I now admired him. I treasured this person for who he was as well as the things he did. I was impressed that he owned a business and seven vehicles; but those things only encouraged me to support him, by being patient and not so needy.

I began to trust him that he was on my team. He always showed up like a superhero, when I was truly in need, and he never led me in any wrong way. He always wanted the best for me, and he had no ego about being my cheerleader. I followed his lead and it led to me being a better person. After some time, I never threatened him again that I was going to leave. I knew I was there to stay; I knew I never wanted to date any other guy. I wanted to learn and grow by his side.

After watching and seeing him I realized the things he found valuable. I valued my money, money is something I do not easily give; but he valued his time, like I valued my money. I would easily ask for his time but did not realize he felt as strongly about it, as I would if someone asked me for money.

There was a time when my finances got off. A situation happened that put me in a rut. During this time, I could not have cared less about snuggling or holding hands. During this time, the matriarch came out in me. I had to hustle and nothing but getting back on top was of any importance to me. This helped me to sympathize. I now knew how he felt in certain seasons when his business thrived. I have a dog named Bae. When I am busy Bae cries a lot. Bae often spends more time in her kennel than she does with me when I am busy. At times I think Bae is mad at me, and sometimes I think she rolls her eyes. When I am busy, Bae's behavior annoys me. I do not have the energy to really care, but when I am rested and whole; then Bae can have all the rubs and time she wants. I am totally available to her.

The new guy may not have time to give me his attention often, but if there is a need he is right there. When I did not want Bae on a chain because she cried and hated it. I took my time and resources and built her a kennel. I may not have time to play but her needs are of the utmost of essence. I go to work to provide her food and I will not rest if there is something she needs, but pats and licks have to come at a convenient time and when that time comes, I will give her all that she needs.

Part two

I began to realize the difference in this man and others, was the difference between love and lust. I got over myself and accepted what he had to give. I had to rewrite everything about relationship, I thought I knew. I had resolved my ego into the fact that things change. It was hard to accept going from my twenties into my forties. My metabolism slowed down, my dexterity was not the same and anxiety showed up, from out of nowhere. By the time I was moving on to fifty, I had embraced my aging changes and saw the wonderful blessings; in having the kids raised, shopping as much as I wanted and finding projects to build, books to write and gardens to grow. Once I embraced it, I realized aging can be bliss.

The thought came to me that I am now more like a green bean and no longer a candy bar, or snack. I was vital to this man and had many things in me that were beneficial to him. Even though adulting was not always fun, I had enough sense to know, I would rather face the challenge and remain green beans on this man's plate; than revert to a candy bar in some man's pocket. Love is challenging, lust is easy.

Love is a sober conscious effort; lust is an easy fleshly desire. Once lust becomes work… it fizzles. When a man sees something inspiring, his first response is not to become erect; his first response is to want to be in her life. Getting me physically will not keep me mentally, but winning my heart ensures the whole package.

A lot of us have not acquired a taste for green beans. After dating and feeling as if it is a futile, repeating cycle. We can apply life to our search for something with substance and learn how to change our tastes, appetite, and desires. I had joined a weight loss program because I was just tired of being tired. In the program I was dedicated to trying new things. Things I had never had a taste for before. The more I ate the healthier foods, the more I desired a taste for the things I did not originally know that I could like. I began to desire and crave the healthy foods and felt weighted down by the old things I used to eat. Once I curbed my sugar intake, sugar became overwhelming to the taste. If we apply ourselves to getting to know men, we would not normally date, we will find that we can develop an appetite for the things they offer. We will also find we do not desire to go back to the old things. It just takes a determination to try new things and an attitude that we are tired of being tired.

I may not be this new guy's candy bar. On the same token, he is not my "Denzel", but I would learn to treat him the same and I figured he could learn to treat me the same.

Part three

Communication is not always easy. Sometimes we express emotions in funny ways. One day I saw my neighbor's dog had somehow got his chain stuck on his foot bone. I went immediately to the dog's rescue, to remove the chain from its foot. Before I knew it, I was screeching in pain. When I opened my eyes, I saw blood dripping at a fast pace from my finger. The dog had bit me!

The dog's intent was not to hurt me. Its intent was to show me, it had an injury; and when I went near its injury, it hurt. Although the dog did need help it was unlikely the help was going to come from me, at that point.

Communication can happen the same way. Someone does something that causes injury and, in our attempts, to communicate, they cause us pain.

We sometimes communicate it in a harsh way. Sometimes it can be so vicious that the other person will no longer want to attempt getting close to us again. Although this man was working hard and there for me, there were times I wanted nothing but his attention. Getting his attention was not going to happen with me beckoning at him. I was hurt because I wanted him and because I was hurt, I would do things to hurt him.

Most people by a certain age have fears. We have gone through many disappointments and developed some triggers. We have to be careful not to assume and label, when we are not getting the things we want. Starting a fight and spewing words, is not productive. Providing false diagnosis to situations will not remedy a cure. Proclaiming he does not care is not the appropriate response. Do not assume a person does not care, because they do not respond how you want them to. Everyone's perception of the right response is different. How a man is groomed to communicate is not how a female is groomed to communicate. Sometimes you may be seeing the other person's fears or shortcomings and making wrong determinations. Sometimes the other person may have triggers, or they may be responding with learned behaviors. Nothing will be accomplished with two people responding from a negative or unrealistic place.

Even once you have the proper diagnosis it may be hard to communicate. Do not get mad or frustrated and speak from a bitter place. Love and relationship are work. Do not become defiant or retaliatory. The dog's intent was not to hurt me, the dog was just communicating the best way he could; but us humans can do better than biting one another with words or hateful actions. Once we figure out our triggers, or things that happened in our pasts; that causes us to react. Once we silence anger and remove any bitterness; that could have formed from past disappointments. We will hear another voice. The voice of our little girl, that is hurt and sad. When we respond to him with innocence, he realizes we need him to kiss it and make it better. When we respond with anger and bitterness, he may think he needs an exorcist.

Communication became easier once I realized that being in a relationship does not make one an expert. Just like giving birth, does not provide us with all the answers, to being a mother. We learn and we grow, and we master….in time.

It's a man's responsibility to make his green beans feel as desirable and fun as a snack and it's a woman's responsibility to be as loving giving and compassionate to that good man as she would Denzel in the Benz with the six pack and wonderful anatomy. Relationships are more satisfying when we learn to get excited about the things, we have to give rather than waiting for someone to make our lives exciting.

Learning how to verbalize my needs gave me the means to eventually get the emotional, mental, and physical support I needed. Admitting your hurt requires vulnerability and allows someone to come in but lashing out is a wall of defense. I began to see my relationship with this man, like I saw interactions with my kids. Sometimes we coddle a baby, spoil them by holding them all the time. Once this is done the baby learns to cry even when they are not wet or hungry. We have taught the baby things that eventually we will not like. Same thing with this man. It works better when we set expectations from the beginning. If we put a baby in its crib and set the expectation that that is where it will be for the night, the baby eventually adheres. When we teach a man, we need his attention, flowers, texts, or phone calls at night; he may push but in the end he adheres. When we set a balance of give and take then he learns and is smoothed into our expectations. I now had what was needed to understand matrimonial love.

Matrimonial love was a component to changing the curse on my family for generations.

The puzzle is finished. When I though on the furniture. God was taking a room in my house and changing it simply by changing the dynamics of the things in the room, thereby rendering the room to serve a totally different purpose. I was great as a single mom, but adding this piece brought to our lives, the pattern set forth by God.

God took a girl devoid and cleaned her up. He clothed her in character and restored her DNA. God gave her purpose and blessed her lineage. A person can be one dimensional, as a flat line, or two dimensional, as a triangle; or they can have three dimensions, such as a cube. I have read a little about the fourth dimension, but my mind could not grasp it. In my searching and seeking, I find that God is limitless; and a scripture that causes me to continue to seek is Ephesians 3:18 and 19. "May be able to comprehend, with all saints what is the breadth, and length, and depth, and height. And to know the love of Christ, which passes knowledge, that ye might be filled with all the fullness of God." I will continue to seek God although my puzzle is finished, and I can see a picture. I know that there is no limit to him and as long as I am alive there will always be new journeys into the fourth dimension.

www.ingramcontent.com/pod-product-compliance
Lightning Source LLC
LaVergne TN
LVHW050539160826
845677LV00011B/2097

* 9 7 9 8 3 6 0 4 3 0 7 6 6 *